If I Were A Butterfly

Kara Lynne Martin

authorHOUSE™

1663 Liberty Drive, Suite 200
Bloomington, Indiana 47403
(800) 839-8640
www.AuthorHouse.com

This book is a work of non-fiction. Unless otherwise noted, the author and the publisher make no explicit guarantees as to the accuracy of the information contained in this book and in some cases, names of people and places have been altered to protect their privacy.

First published by AuthorHouse 11/18/05

ISBN: 1-4208-9679-2 (sc)

Printed in the United States of America
Bloomington, Indiana

This book is printed on acid-free paper.

This book is dedicated to the memory of
Betta Lynn Cunningham,
A Beloved Mother, Grandmother, and
Friend, who touched the lives of many.

To my beautiful daughter Tiffany. I love
you with
All my heart.
"If anyone should ever write my life story,
For whatever reason there might be;
you'll be there,
Between each line of pain and glory,
'cause you're the best
Thing that ever happened to me" Lyrics
by Gladys Knight

And to Matt, who inspires me in many
ways, and always believes
In me, no matter what. I love you Matt.

If I Were A Butterfly

If I were a butterfly, wild and free
Would you admire me? Would you love me?

Trapped in this cocoon, I am not seen
for who I am
I too, want to bloom.

I struggle to get out, and beg you to see
the beauty and love inside of me
I reach out to you and yet am denied
of the support I need or to have you by my side

It hurts so much being trapped in here
when I want so much for you to hold me dear

If I were a butterfly, soaring high
Maybe love for me you would not deny

If I were a butterfly wild and free
I would feel no fear and maybe you would
love me.

If I were a butterfly when I finally saw light,
I would gain my strength
and finally take flight

If I were a butterfly I just want to say
that I would lift my wings, and just fly away

Chapter 1

"Oh God, what's happening to me?" "I can't breathe!" I cried, as I loosened my clothing…unbuttoning the buttons of my brown plaid blouse, and unbuttoning and unzipping my brown corduroy Levi's.

As far as I was concerned, I was dying, struggling for air, my sanity, and my life.

It was a warm afternoon in April. April 28th. 1982. How could I ever forget? I was 19 years old, on the way home from my sisters' house, and I was dying.

I can remember very far back as a young child. I was the middle child of three girls. I have very fond memories of our picnics,

riding our horses, raising rabbits, guinea pigs, cows, etc.
Growing up, I was quite the tom boy, unlike my two sisters.
I spent all the time I could with Dad, whether it was working in the garden, tending to the animals, or out hunting and fishing. I loved the outdoors.
Mom used to "have a fit" as we called it, when Dad would take me in those woods hunting at such a young age, but there was no place I would rather be.
Life was great.

Then the day came when our parents sat us down and told us that Daddy wouldn't be living with us anymore and we were moving into town with Mom.
Devastation set in.
I was only eight years old.
"Why was this happening?"
"We were a family.
Together forever".

Our parents hid it from us a lot when they would argue, and they did what they thought was best.
We had to leave our happy home in the country.

Mom had a nice apartment all fixed up for us before we got there. It was Christmas time and she even had the tree up when we got to our new home.

Mom and Dad continued to try and work things out for a long time, but it never did work out.
I guess Dad still had a lot to learn.

Being in second grade, it was a little scary going to a new school, but I felt welcome there and things were good.
We continued to go with Dad on the weekends and did a lot of fun things.

Mom did her very best. Had a full time job, put the best meals on the table every day, and saw to it that we never went without.

Looking back, I don't know how she did it with three of us, but if there was something we wanted or needed, we got it.

We were all well mannered girls, and both parents did their best to raise, teach, and protect us the best they could, despite the harsh feelings they held between them.

We went to church every Sunday as a family, and after the divorce, Dad saw to it that we were in Sunday school and church twice on Sunday and on Wednesday evenings.

***When I was ten, Dad met Janet, a Christian woman who led him to find the Lord, and his whole life changed.
They are still married today.
Mom met her husband Robert when I was twelve, and they are together as well.***

I had a hard time when my parents remarried. We were all supposed to be together forever, but as I got older, I started to learn and understand more, and came to realize it was for the best.

***Dad was strict, very strict, and very overprotective of us.
Punishments were hard.
Mom would try and get him to go easier on us. Her punishments weren't so tough.
Grounded, and then you were off.
If she was really upset with us, she would threaten to call Dad and that made us behave all the more.***

We were attending the new church that Janet introduced us to. It was a church that she had grown up in.
Her father actually helped build that church.
The people were all nice, a wonderful Pastor and his wife, and we met many new friends there.
This would become the church that taught me more about God, and would lead me to the altar to accept Him as my personal Savior.
From that moment on, God was very important in my life and I was learning more and more about the Bible and how important it is to live right.
Sometimes I was teased by other kids and called names like "Bible Banger", but I didn't care.
I was learning the truth and wanted to keep learning more.

I was a very shy girl, and sometimes our Sunday School teacher or Youth Group leader would ask me to hold the words of hymns up for the other kids, and that actually helped me to interact more and made me feel very special.
One of the songs we sang quite often was "How Great Thou Art". That became a favorite of mine and still is to this day.

I can't hear or sing that song without getting choked up.

Dad and Janet were friends with a couple from our church and they lived on a ranch. They had many horses and cattle. I missed living in the country and on a farm so bad, and they always told us we were welcome there.
Dad took me there a lot.
They had two sons and a daughter and we all became friends. I got to experience and learn a lot by spending time at their house. I saw piglets being born for the first time, watched a rodeo where the horses buck, I rode a few horses, and they even offered to give me the one I rode the most!
I couldn't believe that! I was so excited, but when this was presented to Dad, he explained that where he lived, it was not permitted to have a horse in the township.
I was so hurt over this.
I will never forget that horse. Her name was Sue.
I watched the woman ride her show horse. It was amazing. All she had to do was say a command, and the horse would obey. It was unbelievable!
One day she asked me if I wanted to ride

her show horse.
Her prize winning horse! Wow!
I rode him and felt so privileged and proud.

Life was so great when I would do things like this. I would be so happy.
Then, the weekend would pass, and
I knew I had to go back to school on Monday…….

I was in the fourth grade and my nerves started to get noticeably bad.
In fact, I almost failed that year.
I never told of what was going on in school.
I had a best friend Shelly, we were inseparable, and I always felt bad for her because she was abused at home, both physically and emotionally. But when we were together, we had fun.
The kids were being very mean to us.
They said horrible things, accused us of things, and threatened us constantly.
I was afraid to go to school, was scared to death every day, and almost failed that year.
I never told anyone what was going on. I held my fears all inside.

To this day, I am still affected by the horrible things they did and said. That was the beginning of all my real problems.

When I hit my teenage years, life became very hard for me. It seemed I was so misunderstood by everyone.
Being so close to Dad, I think Mom started resenting that and saw me as being "like him" in many ways.
At first I was proud of that, until I started asking questions and learned of the terrible things he had done and caused in her life. It made me start to resent her saying that to me because it was meant in a negative way, and I couldn't understand why.

I became an outcast……….the black sheep, with my Mom, sisters, and stepfather; always reminding me of how bad I was and never did anything good, or right.
I found myself getting blamed for things I didn't even do.

Life had changed so much.
"How and why was this happening?"
"Didn't they love me anymore?"

Dad never knew what was going on at the house, I never told.
Surely he would have done something if I had told him. But I knew, if I told, and they denied it, I would be punished for lying.
Also, these are the people I love.........I didn't want anyone knowing this and thinking bad of them.
This was my family.

Dad's punishments were tough, but he always showed us and told us he loved us.

At home, why were my sisters being treated with love and praised and I was the bad one?
Where did the love for "me" go?
What could I have done so terrible?

I would lie awake at night thinking through and through what I could have possibly done to make them not love me anymore.
"Was I losing my mind and doing bad things and forgetting what I had done?"
I went on for years thinking I had a brain tumor or mental problem and didn't know what it was.
My anxiety escalated.

When I was in ninth grade, I started

spending a lot of time with my cousin Ally.
She was eight years older than me.
We would go for a lot of rides in her car and go visit friends of hers.
We changed our hangout after a while and started going out to a lake in the country.
This was out in the country where I used to live before my parents divorced.
I really missed the countryside.
We would go to the lake and hang out, play frizbee, meet new people……..it was great.
Every day after dinner she would pick me up, and off we would go to the lake.

While at the lake one 4th of July, there was a kid slightly younger than me on his bicycle.
I recall the day vividly.
I was wearing red pants, a black summer top with skinny straps on the shoulders and red earrings to match.
I was standing there with Ally and a couple guys she had met.
I got to talking to the kid on the bike who had introduced himself as "Matt". He was so sweet and cute, but he was a little younger than me, and Ally and her friends started teasing me.
I liked him, but didn't want to show it much to them because of the teasing.
I had to play it cool.

We were all going to meet at the fireworks not far from the lake, at the park in the middle of the town. Matt said he would ride his bike over and meet me there. He did. We sat in the grass and watched the fireworks, and I was nervous because the hot sparks were falling from the sky and landing on the ground right near where we were sitting, and Matt would comfort me and assure me it would be all right. He was as sweet as ever, but I still tried not to show I liked him as much as I did because of how they all teased me so much.

We continued to meet at "the lake". I gave Matt my phone number, and he called me often.
We would sit on the phone for hours.
He called me from his house, and when his Mom would want him off of the phone, he would ride his bike to a payphone and call me.
If someone needed that phone, he went to another payphone, usually at the lake where we met.
He sometimes called me from school during the day.
Where I went to school at the time, we only went three days a week; three long days, and the other three, I was home, so I was there to take his calls.

We grew very close.
We wanted to see each other all the time, but had to rely on Ally to take me out there in order for that to happen.
When I couldn't get out there, we talked on the phone and started writing letters via postal mail back and forth.
We were in love.
He sent almost every letter in a red envelope that always had S.W.A.K. and 143 on them. (Sealed With A Kiss, and 143 for I Love You).
We spent a lot of time trying to be together, and treasuring every moment when we could be.
He invited me out to meet his family, and I felt very welcome there. They had a nice place out in the country.

We shared a lot; our thoughts, hopes, dreams, and our hearts.

I was having trouble at home, and his Mom even offered for me to come and stay with them for a while.
I never did, but that always stuck in my mind.
What a kind, welcoming offer.

There are many times when I think back

and regret that. As much as I wanted to go, I was just too shy.

The letters continued between us and it became harder and harder for us to be together.
He would ask friends to bring him in, I would ask Ally to take me, but the visits were fewer and fewer.

Every year, they had a fair in the country. I loved the fair! Always went every year. One year I went and was hoping to see Matt there. I thought I would surprise him.

I surprised him all right. He was standing there holding hands with another girl.
My heart sunk.
I was hurt, and I was also embarrassed.
I guess deep down I couldn't blame him because we couldn't see each other very often, but….we were in love!

That put a wedge between us, although he would stress to me how much he regretted "cheating on me".

Our letters continued.

My home life wasn't getting any better.

***I would vent by writing in a journal.
It helped me a lot.
I had that, and my letters to Matt.***

***In August of 1980, right before my sixteenth Birthday, we were all invited to a graduation party out in the country. It was to be an all weekend party.
Mom said I could go, but to be back home at Ally's by 11:00 p.m. and I could go back in the morning.
It was a fun party, lots of food and drinking. I didn't drink, so I watched everyone else make fools of themselves.***

***Matt was there, and I recall his feelings being hurt very badly because I was avoiding him most of the evening and paying more attention to Brad, a guy I had met at the lake.
Even though Matt had done me wrong, so to speak, he still meant so much to me, and I believe I took for granted how he felt for me, just knowing he would always be there.***

***Let me stop here to say "Don't ever take things for granted". It hurts you both in the long run.
Little did I know that after that night, my***

life would change forever.

Matt and his friend gave me a ride home when I left the party.
I stayed at Ally's house that night, and the next day I was getting ready to go back to the party, and a mutual friend of ours, Darlene, was going to take me out.

While blow-drying my hair, the phone rang. It was Matt.
Darlene took the call.
I heard her say……."Brad's dead?"
I dropped the hairdryer in shock. Then she said to me, "No, we were just kidding you; just seeing what you would say".
I said "Don't ever joke around like that again!" I believed they were kidding because I knew Matt was bothered by the Brad thing.

Darlene and I drove back out to the party. There were still people everywhere and Bill, the guy who was having the party, came out to meet us in the driveway. He stated that he had been at the hospital all night. I knew his girlfriend had been ill, so I asked how she was. He said it wasn't her, that two of his friends were killed last night. I said, "They already pulled that joke on me".
I obviously didn't believe him.

He got very upset with me, and walked away.
I was confused at this point.
Two guys from the party overheard this and said to Darlene and I, "We will take you there to the car and prove it's true".
They got in the backseat and told Darlene where to drive.
What I saw when we arrived traumatized me so bad.
The rest of the day is a blank.

The car, the powder blue Duster, was totaled.
There were puddles of blood in the car, their clothing that I recognized right away, Brad's boots……………….

I literally didn't "deal" for a long time after that. Nothing anybody could say or do made me feel better or forget what I had seen.
Going to the funeral home was especially hard, I just wasn't coping.
Why did they take me to that car?
Didn't they know the damage it caused?
Seeing someone your own age lying there in a casket………beyond words.

Sadly, it was all due to drunk driving.

Matt had sent me roses. He was always so

sweet and thoughtful. He wanted me to feel better.
I even remember his Mother calling me telling me how hurt he was and that it seemed like I cared more about Brad than him. I regret him feeling that to this day. I wasn't meaning to hurt him. I just wasn't coping with death, and especially when you're that young and it's someone your age lying there.
I did get counseling for that for years. In fact it was MANY years before I was able to even talk about it without totally breaking down.
Death was just something I couldn't handle, and especially the way I found out, and what I saw that day.

Dad and Janet took me to church camp thinking it may help take my mind off of things.
All I did was cry.
When the other kids tried to convince me that my friends went to hell because they drank, certainly didn't help matters.

My anxiety escalated even more.

From that point on, I had so much fear within me, not realizing it was really fear or what was causing it.

I just knew I felt apprehensive to go certain places and do certain things. I hid this well.

Chapter 2

At home, things were getting worse. I really don't want to get into details for the sake of my family and my love for them.
Just trust me on this, it wasn't good.
My anxiety was escalating and the way I was treated worsened.
My grades were going down in school, I wasn't doing my homework.
I got a whole year of detention for not doing what I was told.
I got the paddle from the principal regularly. That hurt real bad.

I wasn't a trouble maker at all, I just wasn't getting my work done.
I was very quiet and shy in school.
Didn't really have many friends.
I was pretty much a loner.
I was just having trouble concentrating.

I knew the work, I just wasn't getting it done.

My older sister got her driver's license when she turned sixteen, and our stepfather gave her a car.
Since we both went to the same school, she was to take me and bring me home.
I was happy for her when she got the car, and I was also happy because now we could ride to school and home.
I hated that half hour walk to school and back, even when the sun was shining, but it was real awful when it was cold or raining or snowing.
Sometimes my sister would give me a ride, but most of the time, she would leave me and make me walk.
There were times that I would just get out to the parking lot and she would pull away as I chased after her crying, begging her to please give me a ride.
I guess she got pleasure out of doing that to me.
I failed the ninth grade that year.

The following year, I had to switch schools because my grades were too bad to be able to remain at that high school.

My new school was only a block away. At least I didn't have that half hour walk anymore. I was to repeat the ninth grade, but when they tested me, they saw that I knew the work and knew it well, so they put me up in the tenth grade where I belonged. I did know the work, I just wasn't doing it like I should, or doing my homework.

I continued to skip school more frequently. I wasn't doing it with friends, or for any reason except for the fact that I was nervous being there. It was actually SO boring hiding out in the garage all day, and with no lunch. But I couldn't bring myself to go in there some days. I didn't know why, I was just nervous.

Matt and I continued to write letters. I guess I just couldn't get past what had happened between us. My feelings for him never changed though. We may have been young, but what we felt sure was real to us.

When Ally and I would be out for our rides, we would stop and get gas at the Minute Man gas station.

The kid working there was someone I recognized from the first high school I went to. His name was Frank.
He was so shy, but I would talk to him when we went there.
I guess with him being even more shy than I was, it made me feel better and I opened up more.
One day he asked for my phone number, and I gave it to him. He would call me and we would sit there on the phone, never saying a word! We were too shy and had no idea what to say.
I was always getting yelled at to get off of the phone. That used to embarrass me, plus, I never could understand why I was told to get off. I was in the other room, not bothering anybody…..couldn't have, because I wasn't saying much! Nobody else was waiting for a phone call or needed to use the phone. It just seemed that everything I did, I got yelled at for it.

Frank and I started seeing each other on a regular basis. He would walk 45 minutes to pick me up, we would walk to his house, and then he would walk me all the way home later on.
We would hang out, watch TV, and listen to his brother's band practice in the basement. I loved that. I have always loved music, and their band was good.

Sometimes his cousin Tony would take us riding around. I loved going for rides. No destination, just ride.
I can remember getting nervous in the car sometimes and feeling trapped.
One time I begged them to stop the car and let me out to get air. They let me out, but I was so embarrassed afterwards.
I didn't know how to explain what was wrong because I didn't know myself.

There was another time we were with friends and when we came to the train tracks, I flipped out and tried to get out of the car. I thought we were all going to die.

I continued to see Frank and fell in love with him. Our feelings were mutual.
We became very close, wanting to see each other all the time.
I would walk up to the gas station where he worked and spend time with him on the nights he worked. Otherwise, we went to his house or riding around.
He lived at home with his parents, his brothers, and sister.
They were an Italian family. His parents were straight from Italy.
It was interesting for me to learn some of their language and how they would have family over for gatherings, and how different it was.

It reminded me of what I would see in the movies. It was neat.

As for school, I failed again.
Second year in a row.
Not good.
I was missing a lot of school and not doing my work.
Again, they tested me and put me up to the eleventh grade where I normally should have been.
They don't usually do that. Usually, when you fail, you fail.
I clearly knew the work, so they gave me ANOTHER chance.

Matt was still calling me, and he had asked me to go to the movies with him.
He said his Mother was willing to take us to the mall to see a movie and pick us up.
I agreed to go.
He came and picked me up.
Aww, he was so sweet. All cleaned up, smelling good.
We went and saw a James Bond movie.
I really enjoyed that. I always enjoyed being with him.
Ok, now I was stuck. There were two boys here that I had real feelings for.

The next year of school, I was feeling more and more nervous. I kept skipping

school and getting caught, naturally.
One day, the Assistant principal called me into her office because I skipped school again.
I thought I was really in trouble this time.
She got up, and closed the door.
I had so much fear in me, I had no clue what was coming, and she gave me a hug!
I was shocked.
She said "You're having problems at home, aren't you?"
Wow, did it really show that much?

I was having problems at home. More than anyone realized.
I had nowhere to turn. I wouldn't tell anybody, because I loved my family.

To me, it was normal, I guess.
I wanted my family to be normal. Other families had problems, but not mine.

The way I was spoken to and frequently hit was getting pretty severe. I couldn't tell anyone though, they may think my family was bad, and I loved them.
I just couldn't understand WHY.
Why were they doing this to me?
But I wouldn't dare tell anybody about this.

Sometimes the beatings were so severe that I wasn't able to see and my hearing would go in and out. All I could do was cover my head the best I could and take it, and pray until it was over.
My sisters' seemed to enjoy blaming me for things they had done, or telling on me for something either two of us did, or we all did.
And there were times they told on me for things I didn't do at all.

Mom had a habit of threatening to call Dad when I did something wrong, or when she was told I did.
I did NOT want Dad's punishments.
That meant getting hit with the belt and HOURS in the corner. Hands behind your back, face the wall, and no talking.
I remember getting terrible backaches from standing there for so long.
But if I ever said I didn't do it, I got it twice as bad for lying.
I became programmed to admit to things I never did. That happened a lot.

Dad didn't go for wearing stockings, heels, or make up. He especially hated make-up, which included nail polish.
If we got caught, the shoes and stockings went in the garbage, and we had to scrub

the make up off.
Mom said it was ok when we were teens to wear a little make up, but Dad forbade it.

One day, Dad came to school and spent the entire day there following me around to each class making sure I didn't try and put makeup on or smoke cigarettes.
He had me in the principles office in the morning, and made me wash my makeup off.
I was so embarrassed.
I cried the whole day.

Dad was very overprotective, and very, very strict.
In his mind, he was raising us to be good girls, even though the family thought he was a little hard on us.

I can't imagine the rage he must have felt when I was very young, maybe four or five years old and we were visiting our Aunt.
My older sister and I played outside of her house.
We were always taught never to talk to strangers and never ever go inside someone's house that we did not know.

Our Aunt, who was my Father's sister, ran a big apartment complex.
There were probably twenty five

apartments.
In one apartment lived a man, who they considered to be a very kind man, and a friend, and he was babysitting for my parent's friend on a daily basis.
He watched their son David, who was my age.
I was playing with David, who I knew pretty well being that our parents got together all the time, and we went on picnics together, visited each others homes frequently, etc.
David came out of the man's house with a can of pop. The man stepped out and offered me one.
"Yes, please", I said.
The man said "come on in and I will give you some pop".
"But I am not allowed to go in people's houses that I do not know", I replied.
David said "It's ok, he watches me, and he gave me pop".
The man said, "I watch David every day and your parents know me and I know it's ok. If you want pop, you have to come in and get some".
I thought, "yeah, it's ok, if he has David here, I know my parents won't mind".

I went in the man's house, and he told me to come over to him. He said if I wanted pop I had to do what David did.

All I remember is that the man tried to kiss me and force me to do things to him. The next thing I remember is hearing the voice of my older sister, "Kaaaara! Kaaaara!" She was calling me. I left the house and walked back to my Aunts around the corner with her as she was reminding me that we were not allowed in someone else's house. The next few minutes are a blank to me, and what I remember next, is my Dad holding me in his arms in that man's kitchen. My head was over the back of Dad's shoulder and I was looking at the refrigerator magnets, which were fruit, on his refrigerator. I must have told. Dad was asking the man if he touched me and the man was denying it. Dad was highly upset and raising his voice.

Nobody ever talked about it again.

As overprotective as he was, I can only imagine what that did to him. Just the thought of it. As for me, I was very confused. Not sure what had happened there or what it was all about. I had never seen private parts on a man before. I had no idea what that was or what he was trying to do, or why.

As I grew older, the memory stayed with me and I finally understood.
To this day, the thought sickens me to my stomach.

As we grew older, Dad wanted no boys around us. He would not accept it if we had a boyfriend. In fact, he always said "No boyfriends until your Thirty!", and he meant it!

So, here I was, dating Frank. Dad was not happy.
I really don't think anyone was, to be honest.
Matt was very hurt, but in our ongoing letters, I explained the truth to him.
I had feelings for Frank, but never lost any for him.
It was strange.
I was torn.
So, I took it one day at a time.

I continued seeing Frank, but couldn't let Matt go, even if only as a friend.

In school, I found myself feeling even more nervous in my classes.
I skipped school more frequently, and did less and less school work.
I was failing again.

When I DID apply myself and do some work, the teachers would say how good it was and ask why I didn't apply myself more.
I always promised them, and myself, that I would do better.
I WANTED to.
I wanted to be proud of my grades, and to have my parents be proud of me.
I just couldn't get myself to do it.

I wrote in my journal regularly. That became my best friend. But in school, I was so nervous and scared, and didn't know what in the world I was afraid of.
In fact, at the time, I guess I didn't even recognize it as being actual fear.
I felt funny; different.
Sometimes things looked so distorted to me, I felt like I wasn't really there; zoned out or something.
Some days I just couldn't get myself to snap back to reality.
Then when I would go home, I was always getting punished for something, so I could never tell them how I felt.

As it was, they were telling me I was mentally ill, they were going to send me to a psychiatrist, and put me in a home for bad girls.
I used to run to the corner store and use

the payphone and call the home for bad girls and ask them if I really had to come there, and that my family said I am bad and they are going to send me there.
It used to terrify me every time that threat was made.

Not knowing much about the mind and mental issues, and never hearing of anxiety, I started thinking maybe I had a brain tumor or something and that was why I was feeling so uneasy.
I kept all of this to myself.
Either I was going crazy, or I was dying and I couldn't dare tell a soul.
They would have me locked up for sure.
It was awful living that way and not having anyone to go to.

I was frequently called a tramp, and told how I ruined their lives.
How? By existing?
What was I doing so wrong and so bad?

I failed the eleventh grade.
The third year in a row.

I continued to date Frank. I would get very nervous when we would go somewhere, and again, begging them to stop the car so I could get out and get some air.
He and I were growing closer, but I started detecting some real jealousy on his part.

At home the abuse was getting worse. Sometimes I felt I couldn't handle another hit, slap, punch, etc…
Some days I feared the screaming was going to cause me to go deaf.
If we were sitting at the dinner table and I so much as smiled, WHAM! I got it.
My sisters could talk, laugh, make fun of me….but it seemed if I even looked happy or giggled, etc, I was done for.

One day I couldn't take any more. I was being hit, punched in the head and screamed at, covering my head to protect it the best I could from the non stop blows;
I got up and ran out the door.
I called my cousin, where he lived with his wife and two kids, whom I babysat for frequently, and he came and got me and took me to their house to stay for a few days.
I started running more often and going to

their house. They would always call home and tell them where I was and that I was ok.

When I finally would go home, everyone acted like nothing ever happened………. until the next time.

Chapter 3

Being sixteen, the one thing I couldn't wait to get was my driver's license. That is such a big thing when you turn sixteen.

My sister got hers when she was sixteen, and was also given a car.
I was denied of this privilege.
I begged to be allowed to get it, but the answer was no.
That was a hard one for me, for I already knew how to drive.
Dad taught me at a very young age to drive a car, and I couldn't wait until I could legally drive.
All the childhood and teenage dreams that I watched happen for my older sister, and looked forward to for myself, were just that; dreams.

It wasn't going to happen that way for me. I wanted that driver's license so bad, so my cousin took me down to take the exam, and I passed it and my license was mailed to me.
It felt bad sneaking. I hated to feel like I was betraying my mother, but it wasn't fair that I couldn't grow up and experience things that other kids did.
The things we all looked forward to the most in life, I was denied.

I had wanted to quit school and my mother and stepfather told me I couldn't quit unless I had a job.
I went and applied at different fast-food restaurants shortly before school started, which would have been my senior year.

On the first day of school, I went into the office, not knowing what grade they would put me in this time.
The assistant principal suggested I just quit.
I did.
I quit, and walked home nervous, not knowing what they would say when they got home from work.
I wasn't allowed to quit school unless I had a job.

As I was walking in the door, the phone was ringing. I answered it and was asked to come to an interview at one of the restaurants I applied in.

The interview went well, and I got the job.

I was sixteen years old, never worked before, ran a cash register or anything.
I caught on fast, and became good at the register.
The assistant manager once told me I was the most honest person who ever worked for him.
That made me feel so good.

I was very honest, although I was extremely shy and timid and had very low self esteem.

I remember getting my very first paycheck. Ninety dollars! I was thrilled! And the fact that I "earned" that money myself made me proud.

I couldn't wait every day when I got out of work to see Frank. We were getting closer and closer.
I wanted to be with him every minute and it was obvious that he felt the same way about me.
He had a 1968 Roadrunner that he had

bought just before he met me. I thought that was the nicest looking car I had ever seen before.
I was proud to ride in that with him.

Matt and I were still writing letters and I remember lying there at night in bed answering his letters and telling him about Frank and that I still had feelings for him too. It was rough on me, but I was always honest and upfront.

Frank's jealousy got worse and when there was another male around, he was very possessive and would accuse me of things a lot.
I was so wrapped up in him, there was no way I would have betrayed him, but he feared it so bad.
He once told me he was trying to scare me out of it if I were to ever even think about associating with another guy.

When I spent time with him and he brought me home, I would get yelled at if I was late, and usually grounded.
If I was on time, I got yelled at for pushing it, that I couldn't be early, I had to push it to the last minute.
Well, yeah, I wanted to spend every minute I could with him. But getting into trouble for being ON TIME?

The blow-ups got worse at home and it seemed I was always doing something wrong in their eyes. I was just a trouble maker.
My stepfather yelled at me a lot.
If I took a bath and blow dried my hair, etc…it was "noise" and I got into trouble for that too. Once he tried to throw me down the stairs.
Then the day came.
I told Mom some of the things that were going on and he denied it and tried to choke me as I sat in the chair.
Mom tried to get him off of me and told him not to touch me.
He started packing and threatened her, "Either she goes, or I go!" Mom told him he best get packing then because I was her daughter!
I told her I would just go.
One day I would be moving out anyways and I wasn't going to ruin her marriage.

Frank picked me up with my suitcases and I had no clue where I would go from there. I was homeless.

He offered for me to stay at his house, where he lived with his family.
One day lead to weeks, months…….I resided there.
I called home every day. I was so

homesick. I had never been away from home this long before, and I didn't like it. The only thing I liked about it was I got to spend more time with Frank.

His jealousy progressed and he started to become physically violent at times.
He would always apologize and want forgiveness and I would forgive him.

His family rarely stepped in when this would go on.

In time, he started beating me up pretty bad. Black eyes, cuts, unable to move my arm once, had it in a sling.
It got pretty bad.
He would take the mouth piece out of the phone so I couldn't use it, hid my clothes, shoes, make up, etc.... he also broke numerous phones.
Seemed every time one was replaced, it was broken almost right away.
There were times he locked me in the basement all day long with no food, no phone. But he would always apologize and treat me like gold afterwards.
In time, I knew I had to leave.

A year later, I moved back home.
The day I got home, my stepfather told me

I had a week to get out.
I went back to Frank's.

Matt found out what was going on and risked calling me there and begged me to let him help me.
He wanted to get me out of there.

I wanted to go, but yet I didn't, and I always ended up refusing the help.

Frank's sister, Lisa, was married and had three kids.
Her and I got along really well.

Sometimes Frank and I would go to her house and visit her and her husband Denny.
There were times when Denny would pick me up and bring me down to spend time with Lisa and then take me back home afterwards.
In time, Denny started leaving me notes telling me he was in love with me.
"HUH?" That was not normal! This was Lisa's husband, Frank's sisters' husband!
What was this guy thinking???
Plus, everyone knew how much in love I was with Frank.
The notes continued, and then he started calling me on the phone.

I would hide it from everyone because I knew, no matter what, I was going to get blamed.
I was scared and very, very confused.
I never would have dreamed of thinking about another woman's husband especially when they were like family to me!

One day when I was home alone, Denny called. He told me he was coming to pick me up and to have all my stuff ready.
"Was this a joke??"
I then realized he was not joking.
I told him there was no way I was going with him.
He told me if I refused to go, he would hurt Frank's whole family and kill Frank. Said he would break the door down if I did not come out.

He showed up in his Mother's big Lincoln Continental car.
He took me and all my belongings.
The thought of him hurting Frank and his family scared me to death. I would do what it took to protect them so this would not happen.

Denny took me to his mother's house, who lived downstairs from him.
When Frank's brothers came looking there for me, he hid me and made me be quiet until they left.
He then took me to his brother's house and kept me there.

I remember his brother playing the Huey Lewis and the News album.
They fed me and were very nice to me.
Denny treated me as his girlfriend and was very nice to me, kept professing his love for me, yet kept me very afraid.
He would sit there and draw a sketch of me and admire me.
Every time he was near me he just shook, like he couldn't contain how much he felt for me. This was not love, this was sick.

Being young and having an innocent mind, I was just confused by the whole thing.
All I knew was I missed Frank terribly, wanted him to know I was ok, and I wanted to go back.

He took me back to his house where his wife and kids lived.
His wife was now aware and was so afraid of him, she said nothing.
He even had me sleep in bed with him.

I would just cry all night.

In time, his wife revealed she was seeing the kid next door. He was Taiwan and quite a bit younger than her.
So there we all were. It was so uncomfortable and, well, just strange!

Christmas was drawing near. I wanted to go home.
Frank must have been worried sick as to where I was. He ALWAYS knew where I was.
Every so often, I would cry and beg to go home.
I was so afraid.

On Christmas Eve, it was snowing so bad and I was sitting there pleading to go home to Frank. Denny started crying and said he couldn't live without me, and if I left him, he would kill himself.
His wife begged me not to leave. She said he would really do it.
He got a gun and we got it away from him.
He then took pills, enough to kill himself, and I told him I would stay, and took him to the bathroom and made him vomit them up.
He then went into the living room, and just sobbing very hard, he said he didn't

want to lose me and slammed his fist down on the table, and when he did, his hand hit the ashtray and his pinky finger was dangling, almost cut off.
We called the paramedics.

At this point, in walked Frank's mother! I almost fainted. I didn't know what to say or do.
I was so happy to see her, yet I was ashamed and embarrassed.
Would she think I was here all this time willingly??
And what was Frank thinking??

At that point, Denny's mother had come up to the apartment too. Frank's mother said "Come on Kara, Frank is waiting in the car".
Frank??? In the car?? Waiting for me? I am saved!
I wanted to see him SO BAD!

I stood up to go with her.

Then Denny's mother said to her, "She is staying, my son loves her". I stopped.
The two ladies argued, meanwhile, one telling me to come with her and the other telling me to stay and sit down.

I didn't know what to do.

Frank's mother left........without me.

They took Denny to the hospital and fixed his finger up.

The rest is a blurr to me, until the day.........I was crying so hard and wanting Frank, and Denny told me if I wanted to go back that bad, he would take me back.
He loaded all my belongings in the car and was driving towards Frank's house.
I prayed the whole way that I would get there safely.
It was one of the longest rides it seemed. Five minutes, but seemed like an eternity.

When we got in front of Frank's house, Denny put all of my belongings on the curb, I got out and he drove away.
"Oh my God, I was home!" We didn't talk about it much. I always wondered if Frank thought in the back of his mind that maybe I did all that willingly. I can only hope not.
We were all very hurt by it.

Chapter 4

My older sister was to be married, and asked me to be in her wedding. I had never been in a wedding before. I was excited about it. Weddings always made me cry, whether they were on television, or if I attended it. Just the meaning of the vows was so touching to me. This was going to be a special wedding.

On the day she was to be married, I was a nervous wreck. I had those feelings again. The fear, the sweating, the shaking, the feelings of unreality. I went to my sister in all honesty, informing her that I would not be able to bring myself to walk in the church and down the aisle. Instead of support, she threatened me that

if I ruin her wedding, she would kill me.
This made me feel worse.
I did not want to ruin her special day, but I was petrified.

Finally, the Pastor got word of this and he talked with me, opened the window in the church near where I would be standing up front, and told me to picture myself outside in that field that I could view from the window. He also handed me smelling salts incase I felt faint.

I made it through the ceremony. It was so hard, but I did it.
Afterwards, the wedding party was to walk through the nursing home where my sister was employed at the time.
I could not bring myself to go inside that building.
I ended up waiting outside. I just couldn't do it.

At the reception, I went out for air so many times.
I had that feeling of unreality and was full of anxiety.
It seemed like it took forever for the day to end.
I knew something was really going on with me at that point, but I didn't know what it was, or why, and I didn't dare tell anybody.

The jealousy continued with Frank, and the violence got worse.
I got a job working at Arby's.
I liked it, and liked making money.

He didn't like me going to work and being around men.
Sometimes he would make me call in sick, or many times he held me down not allowing me to go in at all.

We got an apartment together. It was a small apartment, but I loved it.
He would leave me there alone a lot and just take off and go to his mother's house.
I would cry the whole time.
I guess he just couldn't let go of "home".
We eventually moved back there.

We went through a lot of other hard times together, as well.

His cousin/ best friend was killed in a motorcycle accident.
He was nineteen, the same age I was at the time.
We both took that extremely hard.
I will never forget the morning we got the news.

Frank didn't handle death very well, and Lord knows I didn't. But I was strong

for him, except for breaking down at the funeral home pretty badly.
We spent a lot of time with his cousin.
Pretty much daily.
We missed him a lot.
We all used to go fishing together every chance we could.

Fishing was one of my most favorite things to do in the whole world.
Once I got out there by the water, it was very hard to get me to leave.
I loved it so much.

I had a dog named Bambi that I begged a woman to sell to me when we had the apartment.
She finally gave her to me.
I loved that dog so much.
I took her everywhere with me.
Then I got a little Siamese kitten I named Timothy.

Frank's parents didn't like dogs, so I really had to keep a close watch on her.
They weren't very nice to her when my back was turned.

One day they let her outside when I was asleep, and she was hit by a car.
She was in the hospital for a long time with a broken pelvic bone.

I went to visit her every day in the hospital. Then, when she came home, I had to carry her everywhere until she was able to walk again.
Bambi and Timothy were best friends.

As for my job at Arby's, I was eventually fired.
I appeared to be irresponsible and that embarrassed me.
He caused me to miss work too many times.
I didn't even attempt to get another job.
I knew what would happen all over again if I did.

The arguing and abuse got worse, I was getting hurt both physically and emotionally, and I felt if it kept up, one day, I may not survive.
I left.
For the final time.

I was there for three years.

I had met a friend at my cousin's named Donny. He was a very sweet person, and we became good friends.
He helped me to get my stuff and move

out, and took me to the Red Roof Inn motel where I, my dog Bambi, and my kitten Timothy stayed.
He came every day and brought food and he paid the bill.
I didn't know where to go. I was taking one day at a time.

My cousin Ally told me I could come and stay with her, but where she lived, they didn't allow animals.

Frank and I were still talking because he was trying to get me to come back to him like I always did when I left.
But this time I didn't.
I moved in to my cousin's apartment.

Frank offered to keep the dog for a while until I figured out what I was going to do.
My kitten Timothy had been getting very sick lately and I didn't know what was wrong.
I had feared that someone had done something to him from the way he was acting.
Poison maybe?

We took him to the vet and they gave him a shot and said he would be fine.
I took him to Frank's for the night, along with the dog.

Timothy was dead in the morning.

Bambi continued to stay with Frank, but when he was at work, she was there with the family. That scared me.

I went to see her every day.
It was killing me.
I had never been apart from her, and once I left, I had nowhere to go except the Motel I was staying in until my cousin invited me to stay with her where I couldn't have my dog.
It was either that, or go back to the abuse.
It was so hard on me.

One day, I went to see Bambi and to take her for a while, and she was gone.

Frank had been at work and he had no idea what had happened.
I begged, pleaded, then demanded to know where my dog was from the family.
All I got was "I don't know".
She was the type that never would have run away. She never needed a leash and always stayed right with you.

Frank was at work and his brothers and sisters were in school.

That left the parents.

I searched the entire city for her.
I put ads in the paper, called the local Humane Society, Streets Department, etc….
No sign of my Bambi.

I was not dealing well at all with the loss of my dog.
First little Timothy, now Bambi.

I stayed at my cousin's house.
Donny and I went for a lot of rides;
I loved riding around seeing the countryside. Sometimes we would stay out all night.
I loved being out.
We would just park alongside a country road sometimes and just sleep there.

My cousin and I would leave notes a lot because we hardly saw each other.
By the time she would get home from work, Donny and I were leaving.

We always had fun just doing whatever.

We ate a lot though.
We always went to the store to buy things

to cook, and would cook it together and eat, and when we were out, we always stopped at a fast food restaurant and got a ton of food to eat.
We both had big appetites.

I remember Mom always wondering if maybe I had a tapeworm because I ate so much.

There was a guy my cousin was dating. He came around a lot.
I was afraid of him.
He always referred to me as "Fox", never by my name. He was a mean man.
Instead of knocking on the door when he came to visit, he would kick it in.
He was very rude and nasty.

When I would take a bath, he would come in the bathroom and stand there. If I demanded him to leave, he would threaten to knock my F'ing head off.
If I reached for a towel to cover up, I got the same threat.

In time, when he would come over, he would tell me to go take a bath, just so he could stand there and watch.
I was petrified of him, had nowhere else to go and nobody to turn to.
I was defenseless to this man. He carried

guns and knives on him all the time. Even the neighbors were afraid of him.

I was starting to feel "weird" when I would go out riding with Donny. Sometimes we would visit his sisters and they were very nice people, but I was feeling uncomfortable. I was starting to get nervous in the stores too. I hid it the best I could.

When Ally and I would ride just to pick up her check at work, I was feeling uneasy. What was going on?

Ally's boyfriend "Steve" came around more often. He wanted to take a picture of me on his Harley Davidson motorcycle in my bikini so he could send it into "Easy Rider" magazine. At first I laughed it off, but then I realized he was serious. I told him no, and he kept insisting on it, until one day, he demanded it and pulled out a loaded 45 caliber pistol and held it to my head. I was so scared, I dropped to the floor right there.

When I was able to stand, I went outside and I sat on the bike and let him take the picture.

***I was feeling that "weird" feeling more and more, especially when I went somewhere.
I was feeling afraid, and I didn't know what I was afraid of, or why.***

***Then the day came…on the way home from my sisters' house.
I was with Donny in the car, it was a warm April, sunny afternoon.
We were at the red light at the intersection, and I remember asking Donny what the fumes were I was smelling. He said it was carburetor cleaner that he had sprayed in his carburetor earlier. I said, "Well, roll down the windows, I don't like smelling those fumes". It made me nervous.***

***The next thing I knew, my world was spinning. I looked around and everything seemed to be swaying.
I didn't feel right.
I tried to hide it and keep it to myself, but it was so overwhelming I could hide it no longer.***

I told Donny something was wrong with me.

My breathing became shallow, I loosened my clothing and begged Donny to get me to the closest place……my Mothers', Frank's, Ally's, just the closest place.

Donny drove fast and kept asking me what was wrong.
I thought I was dying for sure.
This feeling of total terror and panic had come over me, I wanted to get to safety and quick.
As Donny drove, he cried, asking me what he could do for me and what could be happening.
I just pleaded with him to please hurry.

He drove towards Ally's house, and when we got about a block away, the feeling started to gradually go away and I was starting to feel normal again.

I was shaking pretty bad and we were trying to figure out what had just happened.
What was that all about??

We went into the house and decided to

change clothes and put shorts on and go out back in the yard to play frizbee.
I went out back, and when I looked at the house, it looked like it was a million miles away.
I started running towards the back door; it felt like it took forever for me to reach the door.
I was getting that "weird" feeling again! What IS THIS? What's wrong with me? I felt like I was losing my mind!

From that point, the feelings started coming more and more frequently. I was afraid. I was afraid of everything and everyone, except Donny.

I became afraid of looking out the window, talking to anyone who would come over, and the thought of even stepping outside just petrified me.
I don't recall actually telling my family about this, some parts of my life are still a blank, but I do know that when they became aware, they seeked help for me.

My sister called Family Crisis and they sent a woman out to talk to me.

I thought I was losing my mind and they were secretly sending someone to come and take me away and lock me up in a mental institution.

When she entered the house, I ran for the back door. I wanted to run and hide from her.
I got to the door and was afraid to go out! I was trapped!

The woman tried to comfort me, and explain that she was only there to talk to me and it would be ok and she wouldn't make me do anything against my will.
I sat with her on the sofa and told her what I had been feeling.
She had a Police radio in her hand and I didn't trust what she was telling me.
She explained that it was part of her job to carry it, but she would turn it off to make me feel more comfortable.
She did, and it helped.

The woman from Family Crisis contacted a Doctor who made an exception to come out to the house to talk with me.
He was a Psychiatrist.
Ok, now they were showing me that I was crazy!

I agreed to talk with him.
I would have done anything at this point to try and get help and understand why I was feeling this way, and find out what was wrong with me.
He told me I had Agoraphobia.
"Agoraphobia???" "What is that?"
I had never heard of this in my life!

He proceeded to explain the condition to me, and that I was having "anxiety attacks" (Panic attacks).
"Anxiety attacks?"
I was not familiar with anything he was telling me.
He told me there was medication that could control it and help me get over it.
He said sometimes it can take years to overcome this, especially without the medication.
"YEARS???" I cried. I couldn't imagine feeling that way another second, let alone YEARS!

I continued to stay inside, afraid to go out, and had ten to fifteen panic attacks a day. I didn't know what to do, or what room to go in where I would feel the most comfortable when these attacks would occur.
The fear was within me, so I guess I couldn't run from myself, but I sure tried.

I tried every room in the house, then would end up splashing cold water on my face, trying to snap out of it.
Eventually, it would stop, but at any second, another could and would come on out of the blue.
The fear of having another one was overwhelming.

I got books on this and started to read about it.
The books fit what I was going through to a tee.
There were really others out there that went through this? I couldn't imagine.

This fear actually had a name and there were others out there like me! How did they survive? How was "I" going to survive?
Every time I had an attack, I was sure I was dying.

It started becoming somewhat of a joke to Ally and some of the neighbors that would frequently stop at her house.
Sometimes, I would hear "what's the matter Kara? Phobia getting the best of you?"
I knew at that point, nobody was going to help me. I was alone.........living in a hell full of fear.

Chapter 5

Sleep was the only comfort I knew; the only time I was ever at peace, and without all the fear and panic, on edge, just waiting for the next one to strike.
I was afraid to live, and I was afraid to die.

I was always very close to the Lord and would pray to Him all the time.
I started carrying my Bible with me and clutching it tightly when an attack would come on and I would just pray. Pray and pray.
God was all I had to help me through this.

Steve still came around and one time he

brought a prize fighting Pitt-Bull dog and sicked it after me, knowing I was afraid of it.
I ran upstairs and put a dresser in front of the bedroom door and I attempted to jump out the second story window.
The next thing I remember is I ran down the stairs and out the front door, trudging through knee-deep snow in my bare feet and jumped in some man's truck pleading for help.
The rest of that night is a blank.

It seemed people enjoyed torturing me, and laughing at my fears and anxiety.

I was asleep on the couch one day and some of the neighbor boys were over and I woke up with them having the couch lifted into the air while I was on it.
They were trying to scare me.

I didn't dare defend myself from anything anyone did because I was afraid and I needed people.
One time they put an M-80 in between the doors to scare me. It shook the entire block when it went off.
They loved scaring me and getting a laugh out of it.

In time, I became afraid to eat.
I was told they were going to put drugs in my food and I was afraid of drugs or any medication.
I felt weird enough, and was afraid anything I put into my system would affect me and make me feel worse.
They knew this, so they threatened to put it in my food.
They used everything they knew that would scare me to try and make my fears worse, just so they could have a laugh.

I was starving myself. I wanted to take care of myself and stay healthy, but the fear of them "drugging" me was too strong.
Eventually, I completely lost any desire for food. I didn't even feel hungry anymore.
I also developed a fear of having an allergic reaction to food. I read that can happen to people, and I knew if it happened to me, I couldn't leave to go to the hospital, so I was not going to risk it.
I got very thin and weak.
Only weighing 110 pounds at over 5'10" tall to begin with, I couldn't afford NOT to eat, but I was afraid to.
All I could think about was a reaction and them drugging my food.

Mom bought all my food and I knew I had

to eat or I would die. I started to try.
I would take a crumb from a saltine
cracker and put it in my mouth.
If I was ok in an hour, I would take
another crumb.

Eventually, I tried bread; crumb by
crumb. Hours would go by.
The slice of bread would be hard and
stale.

It took months to "try" things, eventually
working my way to hot dogs, baloney,
chicken noodle soup, crackers, potatoes,
and chicken.
Tiny bites at a time, never ever being
"full".

But if someone would walk past my food,
in the garbage it went. Sometimes I would
throw everything away and start with new
food.
I was so empty.
My stomach was empty, my soul was
empty.
All I did was exist in this tortuous hell of
fear.

I kept reading Self-Help books and
learning about the condition and how to
overcome it.

I worked on my eating and looking out the window.
It was so scary, but I wanted to get better so bad.
I learned that doing it, step by step, is what gets you better, but it is so very important to have a support person with you at all times when you try to take steps.
I didn't have that.
All I had was me............me and the Lord.

If I would hear sirens from an ambulance, fire truck, etc....I panicked. Any siren or flashing light sent me into an attack.
I didn't know why......it just did.
I would plug my ears, turn the radio way up, run the water in the sink full blast, pray...........anything to prevent myself from hearing the siren.
I slowly became afraid of just about everything.

I started being told how ugly and stupid I was.
If I dressed nicely, I was asked who the hell I thought I was. I would run and change.
I needed the approval of everyone, didn't

want anyone to ever be mad at me.
I was all alone in this world of fear, and would have done anything to keep them from getting mad at me.
I was told my hair was ugly and it looked like straw and I should get that shit cut off. I liked my hair. Other people always said I had beautiful hair.
Well, they told me it was sickening and they were going to have someone cut it off, and the way THEY wanted it.
I let this happen.
I felt I had no right to stop it, because I needed them.
I cried with every snip as my long blonde hair fell to the floor.

I just couldn't understand why I was afraid to do things that I had done my whole life. Things everyone else was doing; things I WANTED to do.
I didn't understand and neither did anybody else.

The only thing that relieved me was that I learned this was NOT a mental disorder like I thought it was, and it CAN be overcome.

I was determined to beat this thing. This

evil, torturous fear that I was living in. I learned I would not die from it, but as each attack occurred, I believed I was dying.

I would sit downstairs and watch TV a lot. I stayed up all night long quite often. When I would go upstairs to use the bathroom at night, my cousin would yell from her room asking me what the hell I was doing now.
I became afraid to go up there, for every time I did, I got yelled at.
From then on, when I had to use the bathroom, I would hold it.
I wouldn't dare go up those stairs.
In time, I started using a bucket and sneak down into the basement and go in the bucket.
I started having stomach problems from this.
The stomach pain worsened, and I was having uncontrollable bowel movements and all that was pouring out of me was blood and what seemed to look like my intestines.
It was awful and it was scary.
The pain was becoming unbearable.

I told my mother and she came right over. I was crying in so much pain it made her cry.

She called the Emergency room and told them what was wrong and that I couldn't bring myself to go anywhere, and the Doctor told her I was bleeding internally and if I didn't get in there, I would die.

I didn't go.
I prayed instead.

The pain and the bleeding eventually stopped.

I knew I was abusing my body by being afraid to properly take care of myself and nourishing it and cleansing it, but I just couldn't help it.
I was scared.
I wanted to be normal again so bad.

I kept reading the self-help books and trying very hard to look out that window, to be able to have the blinds open.

In my readings, I learned that it is very common for people who suffer from agoraphobia to be sensitive to light.
The more I learned, the more I was finding out that I was not alone.

WOW, OTHERS have gone through THIS too?
It was hard to believe that for the longest time.

I also learned that there were over 14 million people with this condition and only 2 percent actually became completely homebound. (This number is much, much higher today) I happened to be one of the 2 percent.

Matt would pop in to visit me once in a while. That always meant a lot to me, yet I was embarrassed for him to know the hell I was living.
I always tried to act like I was fine, but inside, I was a petrified mess.
Maybe I should have told him just HOW BAD it was.
He would find out later………

In time, I was finally able to stand at the front door and look outside.
I remember having the strong desire to just go out there and touch the grass, trees, sidewalk, etc…. but I couldn't.

Eventually, I was able to step out on the porch for a few seconds, but I had to have the door in my hand, holding it open so it didn't close when I was out there.
I had to know I would be able to get back in right away.

Then, the day came when I was able to stand out there for a couple minutes with the door closed.
The neighbors were over, the ones who hung out there all the time, mostly my age, and when I was outside the door, they slammed it and locked me out.
I totally panicked and ripped the screen trying to get back in.
They got a laugh out of this.
I was embarrassed as ever, but I could not help my fears.
They were REAL.
Meanwhile, I was still asking "WHY?"

People were getting their kicks out of tormenting me.
How could they be so cruel?

I hated every waking moment I had. It was torture to get through a day. Not only tortured by the fear within me, but by those who surrounded me.
I didn't know what I was going to do.

There was nobody to turn to, and I was afraid if I told anyone, I would be treated worse.

I kept taking those steps and going out on the porch, eventually being able to stand out there up to five minutes, then ten……..

There were a couple neighbor ladies who lived across the street, in separate apartments, and when I would work on standing outside, they would yell terrible mean things to me and call me bad names. This made me not want to go out at all, but I knew I had to.

I tried to pick times to work on it when they weren't home.
They called me a bitch, slut, whore, said I was waiting for my next customer, etc…
Why would they talk to me that way?
What could I have done so bad?
They didn't do it to anyone else.

It seemed that everyone was mean to me and out to hurt me worse. Anyone else could stand or sit on their porches and nobody paid any mind, but let me show my face, just once……..I didn't get it.

The glorious day came when I made it off that porch and stepped in the grass in the yard.
I can't even put into words how it felt to be able to feel the sunshine on my face again and to touch God's nature.
I touched the tree, the leaves, the grass and the sidewalk, and I just cried.
I have always loved and appreciated nature and I wasn't able to experience it for so long.
It was beautiful.

Every time I felt I could, after that, I went out and sat in the grass and just touched it.
I wasn't able to walk to the front sidewalk which was maybe 3 feet away, but I was in that yard touching grass!

I lived there at my Cousin's until I was 21 years old. When the landlord found out I was living there with her and her son, he said I had to leave.
That was a nightmare to me.
I couldn't leave!

I was so scared, I contacted the Mayor and explained my situation, and he got them to give me more time.
Meanwhile, I had to check the paper and look for a new place to live.

Chapter 6

I developed Erythrophobia, fear of blushing. I didn't know I had it, or that there was even a name for it for the longest time!
All I knew is if someone looked at me or spoke directly to me that I would blush, kind of like a looking guilty of something blush.
That got REAL BAD.
I avoided people at all cost because of that.
I walked away from people so many times.

I am sure I appeared to be rude or guilty of something, but I could not help it. I was developing more and more fears and phobias that I didn't even know existed at the time!

Frank would still come around and try and get me back. I wanted to so bad, but I knew I just couldn't do it. It would be a big mistake.
Every time I went back, it never changed. It only got worse.
I had to do what was best, even though I wanted him to rescue me.

Steve always threatened that if he saw Frank come around, he was going to kill him. I believed him and made sure he never saw him.

I eventually found an apartment.
Mom and my sister Ann went and looked at it for me.
It would be $185.00 a month rent.
I didn't get that much money.
I was able to get some food stamps and a little money from welfare, but not enough to cover rent like that and the utilities.
Mom said she would help me.

I was not able to go see it or anything, and I didn't know how I was ever going to make it there. I hadn't been anywhere in a year and 4 months.

My older sister's friend gave me some of

her old furniture and other things, and my uncle sold me a couch, loveseat and chair, and a washer and dryer, so I had some furniture.
My younger sister Ann would come over and stay with me on the weekends and she was going to be the one to drive me when I went to the new apartment.

Matt came to visit and I told him I was going to be moving.
Ann was there and they were talking and laughing.
She really liked his car and wanted to go for a ride in it.
I didn't mind a bit, so they went.

Later that evening, she asked me if I cared if she went out with Matt, like a date. I was pretty shocked.
This was the guy that she made fun of me for being so in love with in the past and always said how sickening we were.
I was also embarrassed by it, not sure exactly why, but I just was.
I thought maybe Matt had thought I went looney because of my condition, and...........I had to remind myself of how very HARD he tried in the past and how I hurt him pretty deeply.
But my SISTER?
Oh well, it was not my place to tell either

of them what to do, and I loved them both and just wanted them to be happy.

That same night is when I made the decision to go to the new place.
Ann drove me down and Matt followed.
They tried to make it as "fun" as they could so the fear didn't overwhelm me.
I must say, they did a great job.

We listened to a Don Williams tape and kept playing the song "Lord, I hope this day is good" all night long.

Ann worked at a store at the mall, and she still came and stayed with me on weekends. I always looked forward to that. She continued to date Matt and he spent a lot of time at the house.

A girl I met when I was living at my cousin's house, named Dawn would come to visit me quite a bit. She had moved back to New York State, but we remained friends.
I liked it when she would come to visit and it always made me sad when she would have to leave to go back to New York State.

I had a hard time adjusting to the new place and living on my own. I had never lived alone before. It was strange for me.

***I didn't have enough money to cover the bills so Mom was paying most of my rent and buying my food.
I did apply for SSI, but I didn't hear back from them yet.***

Moving back home was not an option, and that had never been discussed, so I knew I had to make it one way or another, but being alone was bothering me.

***I had a lot of company between Ann and Matt being there a lot and Dawn coming to stay frequently, plus we had some mutual friends that would come and hang out with us.
I tried my best to enjoy it, but I was starting to get those "weird" feelings a lot. What I mean by that is, I would feel spacey, or "drunk", although I didn't drink alcohol at all, I felt like I just "wasn't there".
I hated that feeling, but later learned it was a normal symptom of the anxiety disorder and it was actually your minds way of protecting you when you were***

nervous.
Kind of pulling you out of reality.
It was scary, but I got used to it.

The anxiety, panic attacks, afraid to eat and be alone.........it all became a part of life for me. I was learning to live with it, but it was a constant struggle feeling the terror of fear of so many things that used to be normal things in my life.
I started to wonder "why" I was so afraid of things that were just a normal part of life. Things that people just took for granted every day. Things that used to be normal for me.
I wondered "how" people could feel normal and go places and eat food, etc.. without being afraid.
There were so many times I believed I was losing my mind, and if anyone knew just how I was feeling, they would lock me up in a mental ward.
I hid it as best as I could.

Remembering the threat of drugging my food was playing on my mind pretty badly at this point. My fear of eating was pretty severe.
I was thankful for what I could eat at that point, but was afraid to even eat that, for fear somebody put drugs in it.
I started to ask Ann to eat some of my

food before I would eat it.

I knew if she ate some, it would be ok for me to eat because Ann would never take drugs or anything like that. Every time I was hungry we did this. Whether it was something to eat or drink.

When my food was in front of me and somebody walked past me, I threw it away.

I thought there could be that slight chance that if I even blinked, they could have done something to it.

I starved a lot.

Ann was full a lot because of eating her own meals, then eating portions of my food for me just so I would see it was safe and eat it.

We tried to joke about it, but I was in total fear and she was getting tired of this.

One day when Ann was at work, I was alone and I knew that she would be back by 5:30. Mom always picked her up from work and would bring her to my house.

When it was past 5:30, then 6:00, I started to get worried.

I looked out the window, watching for them to pull up.

I called my Grandmother and told her they weren't back yet.

I started to have a panic attack.

It was a bad one.
I got my Bible and prayed.
I ran in the bathroom splashing cold water on my face.
I never knew what to do to get out of one of these attacks. It was sheer terror.
I felt like I was dying, and it was all within me.
You can't run from yourself, and looking back, I guess that's what I was trying to do.
I would try to find which room of the house I felt the most comfortable in, or what I could do to make this stop.
Eventually, it would stop, and I would just shake for a long time and wonder when the next one would occur.

I lived in fear every second of every day, just waiting in fear, and dreading another one.
I felt for sure I was dying when these would strike.

About an hour and a half later, Ann and Mom walked through the front door. I was crying, and asked them where they were and told them what I had gone through for the last hour and a half.
They said they did a little shopping before they came back.
They couldn't understand why I was so

upset.
I guess because I had expected them, and the normal routine was broken, I couldn't handle it.
CHANGE. It was a change.
That was when I first noticed I couldn't handle change.

After that day, every time I was left alone, I panicked. This got worse and worse each time.
I dreaded Ann leaving the house. I trusted her the most and she became my "safe person".

I later learned that Agoraphobics pick a safe place and/or safe person subconsciously, and this helps them to feel better and not so anxious.

In time, I was so fearful of being alone.
I didn't even know until years later that there was a name for this too.
Monophobia: Fear of being alone.

When Ann had to go somewhere, I would always ask her to tell me ahead of time so I could get someone to come over and be with me until she got back.
It helped, but I was never relaxed until

she got back. I would still panic. Sometimes I panicked even when she was there. Just out of the blue, the feeling would hit me and I knew there was another one coming on.
When this feeling hit, I would yell "Ann!" And she learned in time, that when she heard me call her name in that certain tone that it was happening again.
She would come to me and just hold me. I would hold her tight and put my head on her shoulder until it stopped.
These were occurring more and more often.

Life as I knew it was gone. All I had were memories of how it was to be normal…. to be able to go outside, to be able to eat normally, and to not be afraid of life.
My God, I was afraid of life.
Of existing.
Afraid of every thing around me.
Afraid of everything that had to do with life.
Afraid of my own feelings.
And I was afraid to die.

That was my biggest fear of everything I was feeling.
Of dying.

Each time I had an attack I thought I

was dying. I had no clue as to how this happened to me or why.
I thought when people find out how severe these feelings are, they are going to have me put away in an institution.
Now I thought I knew what it felt like to be "crazy" and losing your mind.

Every day, all day, I was tortured by this fear lingering inside of me. There was no escaping it. I didn't know why, and didn't know what to do.

Chapter 7

Every waking moment of every day was torture for me. These fears had taken over and controlled my every thought, my every feeling. Eating was scary.
Would this ever get better?
I didn't have any answers, only to try and get through each bite of food when it was time to eat.

Every time my Sister had to go somewhere and leave me alone, it was a struggle to get through each moment of every day.

F-E-A-R: False Evidence, Appearing Real. Why was I so afraid of so many things??? Things I always took for granted. "Normal" every day life things.

I was getting frustrated, more confused, and more fearful of more things.

Germs started to become a big factor for me. I didn't even want to breathe the same air as someone else.
I alcoholed the bathroom every day, the phone, doorknobs, etc..
I sprayed Lysol in the room because someone else was in it.

It got to the point where sleep was the only comfort I knew; the only time I was ever relaxed or felt at peace, for every waking moment was torture for me not knowing when the next attack would come and developing more and more fears and not understanding why, or how to make them go away.
The fear was within "me", and I tried to run and hide from myself; there's no better way to explain it.
I found myself sleeping on the bathroom floor, kitchen floor, and even in the walk-in closet in the bedroom.
I wanted so bad to escape the fear and the attacks that so often occurred.
They were within me, there was no escape.

When my friend would come to visit from New York, I would beg her to stay. Sometimes she would be there for a month or more at a time.
When it would come time for her to leave, I would cry and panic.
She would have to drive around the block until she knew I would be ok for her to actually "leave".
If she came around and I was still standing in the door, she would drive around again, and keep doing that until she didn't see me standing there anymore.
That was her sign to go ahead and start for home in New York.
It was never actually "ok" for me to let her go, but I knew I had to work myself up to accepting the fact that she was leaving.

I found that doing something very active would help me. I would get out a bucket and start washing the floor. It helped me a lot.
So, many times when I felt anxious, or there was going to be a "change", I would get out my bucket and start washing floors.

The majority of the time, I had that feeling of unreality. Like I wasn't really

there.
It's a strange feeling to go about your day, you are functioning normally, but you feel like you are in the clouds or something.
I often wondered what it would feel like to be normal again.
To feel normal reality, to go places again.
Just to exist normally without all this fear and torment of panic.

Ann would have to hold my hand when she got my mail for me. I would stand inside the house and she would reach out the door to get the mail out of the box. I would ask her to promise me she would not let go of me while she did this.

When I went to the bathroom, took a bath, etc… she had to be right there with me and vice- versa. I didn't want to be alone or I would panic.
Not sure what I would have done if she hadn't agreed to support me in this way. I was not coping well at all.
I was going crazy on the inside.

On New Years Eve, Ann and Matt were invited out to some friend's house in the country to attend a New Years Eve party. I wanted them to go and have fun, but I

knew I couldn't handle it if they left me home alone.
I called people to see if someone would be willing to sit with me while they were gone.

Finally, my older sister and her husband agreed to come sit with me so Ann could go for a while.
Ann and I worked it all out with her that they would stay with me until Ann got back from her party, and if for any reason they had to leave before Ann got home, to call and give Ann enough time to get home. Ann agreed that if we called, she would come home immediately.
I was having a hard time being away from Ann, but I struggled to be "ok" knowing she would be coming back home in a few hours.
Well, shortly after she left, my sister that was staying with me decided she was going to leave.
I begged her not to for she had PROMISED to stay with me until Ann got home.
I asked her to please at least let me call Ann and give her time to come back home. After all, we had it all planned and had everything covered.
She refused to wait.
I called Ann, and she said she was

starting right back for home.
I told my sister that was with me and begged her to wait.
They got their coats on and continued getting ready to leave as I panicked and begged them not to leave me. I even got on my knees before them, begging them, and pleading with them not to leave me.
They stepped around me and went out the door.

It's hard to even put it into words what was going on inside of me right then.
How could they do that to me?
They lied to me and, they didn't care that I was panicking and begging them not to leave me.
They PROMISED ME!

That was a bad night.

How could I ever feel content or trust anyone again?
I ran to the phone and called my Aunt and Uncle who lived the closest to me.
I was crying and telling them what was going on and that my sister had left me.
My Uncle stayed on the phone with me until my aunt got her boots on and they came immediately to my house and stayed with me until Ann got back.
I will never forget that as long as I live.

And to answer any questions that "Maybe" they were trying to help me by causing me to be strong to show myself that I could handle it, the answer is absolutely NOT.
It was cold and it was heartless.
There was no concern or caring for my well-being intended there at all.

My cat had kittens and there was a little orange kitten that my friends' son had accidentally slammed in the cupboard door in the kitchen. He was hurt and sick and almost died.
I cared for him, became very attached, and vowed that I would keep him forever.
I loved him so much. He was my Petie.

That kitty was on my lap or in my arms all the time.
He was my boy.

Some time later, the cat had another litter of kittens and there was one who was born partially paralyzed. She dragged her back legs, but she was in no pain and she was happy and healthy. I had to care for her a lot. I enjoyed it. It gave me purpose and I loved her.
My older sister kept telling me she was

crippled and I couldn't keep her that way.

I was so weak-minded and needed people so bad that I wanted their approval all the time so they would never get mad at me and not come around anymore that I allowed her to come in one day and take her away to go have her put to death.
I took that very hard. It was like I had no say so.
She was my kitty, I took care of her and I loved her.

I couldn't see it at the time, and even if I did, I allowed this to go on because I needed people so bad and I feared someone getting mad at me.

Believe me, I look back on those things and I have many regrets, and many, many hurts.
I can see the whole picture of just what was going on. They were deliberately controlling me and hurting me.
To this day, I will never understand how people can get any sort of satisfaction out of things like that.

Frank would come around a lot and harass me and threaten to drive his car

through my house. It caused a lot of upset in the neighborhood.
That lead to me getting evicted.
I only lived there for 8 months when this happened. I wasn't even adjusted to the new apartment yet, and I had to leave.

I started looking in the newspaper for apartments for rent.
I found one up in a nice neighborhood where I always wanted to live.
The rent was high and Mom said I would never make it there.
I wanted it so bad. They looked at it for me and I made the decision to take it.

I was 21 years old at the time, and was happy I was moving to that particular neighborhood, but scared to death because I was moving again and had to readjust to a new atmosphere.

I was dating a guy, and he helped to move my belongings to the new apartment. Just like the first apartment, I never saw this one until my things were all moved in, and I came last.

It was scary getting there, but I must say I was very pleased with the apartment.
It was well-kept and I liked it a lot.

When I got there, my boyfriend had the curtains up for me, and the furniture all set up. It looked just like a home.
I knew somehow the Lord would just work it out and I would be able to make it with the rent and the bills.
If you have faith, He will always make sure things work out.

Ann stayed with me a lot there, and when she wasn't there, my boyfriend was there a lot.
I felt safer because my landlords lived right downstairs from me and they were a real nice young couple.
Just knowing someone was there, helped me to feel more secure, although being alone was still very hard.

The guy I was seeing drank a lot of beer and he started getting nasty to me at times. I didn't understand it.
He knew I had been in an abusive relationship and claimed he thought that was so terrible and would tell me how he couldn't understand how someone could treat me that way.
Well, then how could he?

I continued to work on going outside. I sat on the porch a lot and would walk around on the sidewalk in front of my house.

***I was getting counseling once a week.
They would come to my house.
Sometimes we sat and talked and
sometimes we ventured outside to try and
get me to walk farther.
I would take it one step at a time.
Eventually, I was able to walk the distance
of one house away, then two…..***

***Traffic bothered me very badly.
I was afraid of the cars, always thinking
they were going to hit me and kill me.
And if a strange man walked by, I also
panicked and would run in the house,
thinking he was going to hurt me.
I trusted no one but my sister Ann.***

***I eventually made it to the shortest corner
on my block near my house.
The side street there was a busy street with
lots of traffic.
I was very afraid of this.***

***Ann would walk with me and we would
stand there and I would put my head on
her shoulder and close my eyes while the
traffic went by. This is how we were trying
to get me over the fear of the traffic going
by.
Gradually, I would lift my head and look
at the cars.
It took a long time before I was able to***

handle walking to that corner alone and facing the traffic without panicking or running home.

To be in a car was another fear.
We would sit in the car in the driveway and I had to keep the door open.
In time, we would sit with the car running, then closing the car door.
Then we sat in it in the street in front of the house. But when a car would go by us, I would panic and cry saying "They are going to kill us!" I was petrified.
We worked on that a lot and it did get easier for me.

There was a store on the corner of my block, the longest corner from my house and I could not walk that far.
When I needed something, I would have to ask someone to go for me.
Mom did all of my shopping, but to get something from that store, I used to pay the neighbor kids to do it for me.
I wanted to be able to go there so bad myself, but I just couldn't.

I walked back and forth out front over and over every day just trying to get even an inch farther from my house.

I was determined to get better.
I was not going to accept what was happening to me. I wanted to feel normal again and I wanted my freedom back.
Freedom from the fear that was torturing me every waking moment.

I broke up with the guy I was dating.
His abuse got worse, and I ended the relationship.
I was afraid of him, but one day I got strong and went right up to him and told him it was over. I was tired of being mistreated and lied to.
He was also a very jealous, controlling person, and I knew he was trying to hold me back from getting better and going outside.
That was the last thing I needed in my life.

I worked on my eating, and was able to eat more foods.
I wasn't panicking constantly anymore while in the house. I would still feel real spacey and I hated that, but the attacks were less.

As long as I knew my neighbors were home, I felt better, but when they weren't, I would feel anxious until I saw them come home.
However, if I would hear a siren outside, I did panic. I would call my Grandma and tell her I heard a siren and she would try and calm me as I panicked, going from room to room, Bible in hand, and praying. She would hold on the phone while I went into the bathroom and splashed cold water on my face to try and snap myself out of it.

If it happened, and I couldn't get a hold of anyone, I would turn the radio on real loud, turn the water on full blast….. anything to drown out the sound outside so I didn't hear it.

Sirens and flashing lights meant something "bad" had happened, and I could not handle the thoughts of that.

It was strange for me to be home all the time, considering how I was always on the go before this happened to me, but I found ways to occupy my days.
I loved music very much and would just get lost in it for hours at a time. I had many tapes, and I would sit on the floor in front of the stereo and listen to favorite

songs.
My cat Petie was always with me and I talked to him all day long. I couldn't imagine not having him.

I loved children very much and the neighbor kids would come to visit me almost daily.
They would ask to spend the night a lot and they took turns doing that. I enjoyed having them around.
Different people would ask me to babysit for them a lot too, seeing I was home all the time.
My days got busier with the kids and it made me feel good to do this. It helped the parents out and it made me feel I had some worth.
I was good with kids, I must say. I just had a way with them, and they loved me, and I loved them.
I wanted one of my own very badly. It became my dream in life…….to be a Mom.

I was watching three kids for a couple who lived up the street from me. They were beautiful kids.
One day their father said "Kara, you are so good with the kids, yet you can't even

cross the street. I don't understand." He wanted to help me, but just didn't know how, or have the answers. Neither did I.

One day he came to me and told me of an article he saw in the paper where someone was doing a Seminar on Anxiety and Agoraphobia, and there was a program you could buy consisting of Cassette tapes and worksheets.
He offered to buy it for me, and I told him that was very kind, but I just didn't see how listening to tapes was going to help me.
I was very negative about that.
He insisted, and asked me if he bought the Program, if I would at least be willing to "try" it.
It was a very expensive program, and I felt guilty that he was spending all that money on me, but he did get it, and I tried the program.
It was the program for stress and anxiety. One tape a week came in the mail to listen to, and worksheets to do.
I learned a lot. I learned that I am not the only one who suffered from this, and the ways I would feel, others felt like that too. I wasn't alone in this.
I learned, in order to get better, we have to change our way of thinking.

Stop thinking so negative and build up some self confidence and self- esteem, and the support of people close to you is so very important.

One day, when one of the young neighbor girls was over visiting, I went into the bathroom and the doorknob fell off.
I lived on the second floor and there were no window in my bathroom.
The part of the doorknob with the long part that sticks into the hole fell on the outside of the bathroom.
There was no way for me to get that door open, to get out of that bathroom.

I started to panic, beating on the door and screaming.
I thought I might die right then and there.
It was an awful feeling.
I screamed for the little girl to come to the door and stick the end of the doorknob into the hole and turn it.
Thank God she was there that day. If she hadn't been, I can't imagine what would have happened or when I would have ever been found and let out of there.
I developed a SEVERE case of Claustrophobia from that day on.

I continued to go through the program with the tapes and reading other self help books. I read and learned all I could.
I wanted to get better so bad.
Time was passing quickly and I was getting older.
I wanted my freedom back.
I wanted to stop feeling this way and experiencing the torturing anxiety that was crippling my life.

My family became less supportive and I would rely on knowing the neighbors were home to make me feel better.
I would look out the window to make sure I saw a car in the driveway, etc.
Just knowing someone was nearby in case I "needed" help made me feel more content.
Never totally content, but it did bring me some peace.

I was frequently screamed at and called bad names. I would end up crying every time, asking what I did so wrong.
I used to get treated like this at home, but now I was an adult and was out on my own, living in my own apartment.
Would it ever stop?

Sometimes I would get so upset over it, that I did not deal well. I would have to call a friend who would try and comfort me, or they wouldn't be able to calm me and have to call a Pastor or Family Crisis to talk to me and calm me down, reassuring me that I did not do anything wrong, was not stupid, and didn't deserve being treated that way.

This happened more times than I can ever count.

It happened outside in front of people too, which really embarrassed me.

I can recall my landlady standing in the front door shaking her head and crying, asking me what I ever could have done so wrong to deserve that. She said I was such a nice person and kind to everyone. I was. So, why?

I was constantly put down as a human being.

Chapter 8

I had a friend who used to date a girlfriend of mine who would visit me when he would come to town. He always remembered me and that made me feel good.
He would write letters every so often and call me once in a while to keep in touch and come over.
We always had fun visits.
He made me laugh a lot.

One day he called to say he was back in town for a few days and asked to come over. I was very excited.
He asked me on the phone if I was home alone or if I was expecting anyone else to come over. I thought that was a strange question, but I knew how sometimes he could be shy around people and thought

maybe that was the reason he asked.

He came over and we were talking and laughing like usual, then he came over to me and tried to touch me.
I didn't know how to react, so I sort of chuckled and asked him what he was doing. We were always friends, nothing more, and this was not like him to do something like this.
He got a little pushy with the physical contact, and I became very uncomfortable at this point.
I got up and walked away from him, but he was very persistent.
He ended up raping me.
This lasted all night long.

I always used to wonder how a woman just can't get away from a forceful man, but after struggling for hours, I became exhausted and withdrawn.
He held me down, wouldn't even allow me to get up to use the bathroom, and repeated the act a second time.
It was horrible.

When morning came, he finally left.

That morning happened to be Easter morning, and my family was coming over for Easter dinner.

I was beside myself.
I didn't know what to do. I was afraid to tell anyone, yet I wanted to.
I needed comfort.
It had been my time of the month, and there was a mess on my living room furniture where it happened.
I scrubbed the furniture, and when the family came, I told them I had spilled kool aid and that was why the cushions were still wet.

A few days later, I did call a rape crisis center, but after talking to them, I decided I wasn't going to give them my name.
I was ashamed, embarrassed, and I thought if anyone found out, they would blame me.

I was always getting blamed for everything, and after losing my self esteem and confidence over time, I thought it wouldn't matter to anyone because "I" didn't matter.
I believed I was worthless and had no right to have rights.

When a neighbor or friend would compliment me on anything, or tell me I was pretty, I would tell them they were

just saying that because they felt sorry for me. I couldn't even bring myself to sit there and have a conversation without eventually walking away or hiding my face, putting my back to them, etc... because I truly believed I was ugly and I didn't want them to see.
I would cry a lot and run away.
I could not help these reactions.

I was receiving counseling once a week, but it wasn't helping me.
I would sit and talk about the past and what I was feeling, but I wasn't getting any better.
After 5 years of it, they told me I didn't need them and that they were learning from me.
They weren't experienced with Agoraphobia, and I would tell them of all I learned and read.

I knew what had to be done to overcome it, but I was having a hard time doing it. I didn't have the support I needed.
My family was getting tired of hearing it and dealing with me.

I learned that getting out there and doing it, step by step, and that the love and

support from family and friends played a big part in recovery, but I didn't have that. I would do all I could to try and recover on my own, but there was only so much I would attempt alone. So, when they said I didn't need them, I had to agree.
I could sit there and talk about it all I wanted, but I needed that hand to hold, so to speak, and someone to go with me to take these steps while trying to recover.

I would pray all the time hoping God would send someone who's heart was really in it to take the time to help me; to go with me, and hold my hand as I tried to walk further, cross the street, etc…

There were people here and there who would offer to help me, but it appeared to me that they were only trying to be a "hero" so to speak. What I mean by that, is they would walk with me a few times, but if I didn't get over it right then, they wouldn't help me anymore.
Some people just don't understand the condition, and, or maybe just don't have the patience it takes, and if I didn't get to the point or make the goals "they" had set, they gave up on me.
Didn't they ever stop to think that when they were out shopping, going to work, the beach, etc…that I was still sitting there at

home?
Years were passing me by.
If only someone would take the time for me, I could get better! I would be able to do those things again too.
From every story I read or learned about someone recovering, they all had someone who helped them on a regular basis and supported them and they got better.
Oh, how I prayed for that person to come along. Meanwhile, I tried and tried to overcome this myself.

With developing so many different phobias, the eating disorder, and the obsessive compulsive behavior, I had a lot to battle. In most cases, people develop one of these things. I had them all.
I was completely alone with this terror I lived with. Meanwhile, trying to act like I was ok because of the fear that my family would have me locked up in an institution for the rest of my life thinking I was crazy.

I contacted many doctors asking what kind of help was out there, and if in fact, they would be willing to help me.
Some doctors strongly recommended medication, others said they strongly recommend NOT taking medication because it is highly addictive.

I was so afraid of things, I wouldn't even take an aspirin or a vitamin, so there was no way I was taking medication.

The only doctor that agreed to help me with my problem told me if I didn't take the meds, he would no longer help me. That ended that. I couldn't bring myself to take a pill. It was totally out of the question for me.

At this point, I didn't know what I was going to do other than to keep on going outside and walking back and forth on the sidewalk trying to get even a step further. It was clear, I was alone in this.

My neighbors weren't very friendly with me. Most of them just stared when I would be outside. I could feel the cold stares, and knew they whispered and talked about me.

I tried to be friendly and always spoke and said hello.
"Why couldn't people see me for who I was and give me a chance?"
I could never fit in with anything.
Not even socializing with neighbors.
It seemed I was always rejected.
I cared about people very much, why

didn't people care about me?
This would bother me a lot.

I continued to go outside and walk and try to get further. It would take weeks before I would get even another step further, but it would thrill me because it was ONE MORE STEP!
I still prayed for that one person with the time, patience, and compassion to come along and be that hand to hold for me.
Would it ever happen?
It sure didn't look promising.

It's not that I depended on someone else to get me better. I knew that the problem was within me and I would be the one to have to do it, but that support of someone was so very important.
Every other recovered agoraphobic had someone….a husband, boyfriend, family member, etc… to support them and go with them and hold their hand through this. Having someone with you makes all the difference.

People were slowly giving up on me. Either I didn't do what they wanted me to do in the time they expected, or they just didn't care.

This was hurting me bad.
Surely they would have to know that I wanted more than anything to recover from this.
Nobody in their right mind would "choose" to live like this. And not only was I living like this, but I was being tortured on the inside by the constant anxiety and worry and the awful panic attacks that would strike me out of the blue and cause me to think I was losing my mind and/or dying.

A doctor that some members of my family went to told my mother he wanted to help me.
He felt he could get me over this.
I was thrilled to hear this and I accepted the help.
Was this the answer to my prayers?

He called me and came over to meet me.
He was a young, handsome man and he seemed nice, yet I detected something "different" about him, but I just couldn't put a finger on what it was.
I tried to chase the negativity out of my mind and replace those thoughts with positive ones.
I "needed" the help desperately, and he

was there offering it to me.
He called me, and came over to see me a few times and wanted to start venturing out for rides.
We started around the first block, and I was actually doing quite well. I had a lot of anxiety, but I wanted to beat this thing and get better.
We ventured out a couple times a week. Always in the evening, because it was worse for me in the day to go out, for there was more people out and about, and the traffic was heavier.

I didn't trust people. Even when I would be out for a walk, if I saw a strange man walking by, I ran in the house. All I could think, is he was going to do something to me that was harmful.
Trust was a hard thing for me to have in people, but I needed people to help me get better, so I tried the best I could to have that trust.

My rides with the doctor continued.
I had a fear of getting into a car accident real bad. Ever since that accident when my friends were killed right before my sixteenth birthday, I feared that happening to me. It was a hard fear to get over for this is something that "can" happen. It's not like it was something that

was not possible to ever happen.
I spent more time obsessing on the "what if's" than anything else. But I still fought the fears and went while I had the help that I prayed so hard for.

One day when "the doctor" came to pick me up, I told him I had to go get my glasses and my house keys and I would be ready to go. He waited in the living room for me. When I returned, he was lying on my couch completely nude.
I immediately turned around, facing my back to him and asked him what in the world he was doing. He replied that there was nothing to be ashamed of, and when two people liked each other, it was normal to "be together".
I asked him to please get dressed, and told him I thought he was there to help me.
He got dressed, apologized, and still wanted to take me for that ride.
At this point I knew I didn't want to be around him. I felt he wasn't there to "help" me. It wasn't in his heart. He was a man, and wanted something more, but it wasn't out of feelings for me either.

I knew it would be wrong for me to go with him again, but I had PRAYED so long for the help.
My desperation to get better, knowing he

was my only help, made me go with him for that ride.
I did make it clear to him that women may "fall all over" him all the time and look at him like "the rich, handsome doctor", but to me, he was a person, no better than anyone else. He smiled and said that was what he liked about me, and that I was unique.

I tried to put that incident behind me, but I was never completely comfortable with all of this.
My desperation to get better kept me going for those rides with him.

I was making progress and was thrilled about this.

One evening, I got further than I ever had before. I was several blocks from home and he told me if I went just one more block, he would turn right around and we would head back. I believed him because he always gave me his word, and so far, he had always kept his promises.
When I wanted to turn around, he always did, so I felt ok with this.

We were to go to the end of the block, up

around the boulevard, and head back towards my house.
When we got to the end of the boulevard, he didn't turn back up, he made a left hand turn on to the busiest street, the one he knew I was petrified of.
I think he was trying to be a "hero" and force me to do it so he could say "See? You did it".
No. It didn't work that way, for my condition is "real" and force can only set you back and make you lose trust in people all the more.

I started asking him what he was doing. He ignored me. I started to panic and scream "You promised me!" over and over. I thought I might die right there. I cried and screamed at him and took off my leather boot and threw it at him.

He finally turned around and apologized all the way home while I hyperventilated and tried to regain my composure and calm down.
He begged my forgiveness and told me he would even give it to me in writing of how sorry he was and assure me that it would never happen again.
He did give it to me in writing, but at this point, I had lost total trust in him.

He continued to call me and stopped over again, and when I answered the door, he tried to touch me sexually and said things that were inappropriate in a sexual manner. I asked him to leave.

He sent me flowers for my birthday and would call wanting to see me and help me. He even asked me to move in with him. He told me my house was a cardboard box and I would be happier living at his house, which was huge with maid's quarters, seven fireplaces, etc…
I took offence to that.
That "cardboard box" he spoke of was MY HOME.
I had a nice apartment, and how dare he say something like that to me. I asked him to never call me again.
He told me I "needed" him and would never get better without him. I assured him I did not need that kind of help and to leave me alone for good.
My family was very upset to hear of this, and they all stopped going to him.
I was glad, for this man had fooled all of us and was not the person we thought he was.
I knew better from the start that I shouldn't have allowed him to come around that long, but I wanted to get better so bad. I thought maybe it was a test

in life or something to see just how bad I wanted to get better.
Naturally, I wanted to get better real bad, but I wasn't going to allow things that I knew were morally wrong to go on. This man was not a good man.

There I was, at a stand still again with no help, no vehicle to work on getting out, even if I wanted to attempt it alone. And with less trust in people than what I had before, which wasn't much to begin with. I was hurt by this and another scar was added.
I couldn't understand why people just couldn't genuinely "care" about another human being. Why they could pretend to care, but have other selfish reasons behind it all.

I asked my family members quite often to walk some with me or take me just around the block once in a while. They told me they were tired of hearing it, they didn't have the time, and they were sick of hearing me complain.

Didn't they understand?
I was sitting there day after day and that would be what it took for me to get better.

I was begging for the help.
They made sure I always had food and what I needed, but I also needed my freedom back.
I wanted to go to the beach again, go shopping, go to the Zoo again…………

I learned to enjoy my own company, which I was thankful for.
My family didn't visit me as often as they were at first, but always came over on the Holidays.
I think if I didn't learn to enjoy my own company and occupy myself, that I would have gone crazy.

I was still very much into music. I had a wide collection and could just get lost listening to it for hours at a time.

My anxiety was still a frequent thing and some days were worse than others.
I felt that spacey feeling a lot, and had panic attacks quite often.
I started to get depressed and felt that I would never get better or escape these feelings that tormented my every waking moment. I was suffering badly from this and nobody understood or wanted to help me, and people had less and less time for me.

Chapter 9

I felt like I was a burden to my family and was just taking up space in this world.
I had lost all my self esteem and confidence and I no longer wanted to live.

I was never one to be suicidal, but I couldn't handle living in this fear any longer.
Every second was a struggle to get through, and it seemed sleep was the only comfort I knew.
I thought about it for about two weeks to make sure it is what I wanted, and when that was confirmed, on how I would do it.
I thought about turning on the gas and going to sleep, and about shooting myself.

I didn't want to harm anyone else in the area, for my landlords lived downstairs from me, so I decided I would shoot myself. I was very calm about this decision and felt it would be my only escape.

I phoned my friend Dawn from New York and calmly told her of my decision.
I wanted her to know because I was the closest to her, and she lived so far away, and she would have a hard time finding out what ever happened to me.
When I told her, she cried hard and begged me not to do this.
I told her why I made the choice I made, and she told me to sit and think about how selfish I would be and of the people I would be hurting.
I told her that I felt people would be relieved because I was such a burden to them.
She told me to think harder, and as she named off names, to picture those people standing over my casket. I did, and boy did I change my way of thinking.
I never want to hurt anyone! Especially like that!
I guess I was being selfish, but I wanted to escape this terror I was living.

I am thankful to my friend to this day for

opening my eyes as to what I was about to do. Plus, it is a sin to the Lord to take your own life, and I knew that I wanted to go to heaven when I died and have eternal life in peace.

As much as I struggled every waking moment to "live", I wanted to end it all and die.

That was a tough state to be in.

But, I loved my family more than I loved myself.

I would struggle to live to spare them the pain and heartache that I sometimes thought they would feel if I were to die.

Other times, I kind of questioned that.

"Would they really be hurt? Maybe just relieved…..?"

Either way, it was a sin in the eyes of the Lord, and I really loved the Lord. I tried my best to stay close to Him and lean on Him and to live right.

I would ask Him often why this was happening to me. I would sit and think and think what I could have ever done so bad to deserve this. And if I didn't deserve it, why He allowed this to happen.

I was a good person. I loved others and treated them with respect. I never committed any crimes.

I knew, in order to overcome this, I would have to have faith and that is something I struggled with.
To me, having faith like that is like falling backwards into an open flame and trusting someone will catch you. It was hard for me.
I didn't mean to question the Lord's Word, but I was.
I went to Him with everything, and I wanted so much to have that total faith.

When Jesus told Peter to walk on the water and focus on Him, Peter started to walk, but when he looked down and became afraid, he started to sink. When he asked Jesus why he was sinking, Jesus replied that he told him to focus on Him, and he doubted Him, and began to sink.
I read my Bible all the time, and I knew what it would take, but I still struggled with this.
Sometimes I would contact a Pastor from a church and talk to him about my struggle with keeping the faith. They always told me it was a struggle for everyone.
It is hard sometimes, but when you have it, miracles can happen.
I continued to try, and there were times I did have unbelievable faith, and things happened.

I would do things I never thought I could do, but then I would get scared.

"Trust in the Lord with all your heart and lean not on your own understanding". I would tell myself this over and over.
"I can do all things through Jesus Christ who strengthens me". I even wrote this on an index card and would take it with me when I went out for a walk.

I wanted so much to lean only on the Lord. If I could do that, He would see me through. But still, I kept failing.

I would get scared and the "what if's" would enter my mind. The what if's were like a disease to me. I couldn't chase them away for I knew they were things that really COULD happen! How was I going to forget about the possibilities?
Things I feared the most could very well happen.

I started to wonder how other people could just live their lives without the fear of the what if's.
It had been so long since I felt normal, without anxiety, or went anywhere, that I wondered how other people could do it. How they could just get in a car and go shopping, or to the beach.

The thought of it terrified me. Then I would fear for them, thinking that I could once go places and do anything I wanted too, but now I know that panic can strike you without warning at any given moment, and there was no way I could risk that again. I suffered enough even being in the house.

The thought of going too far was very hard for me. I kept reminding myself of what could happen, just to protect myself from going too far and having it strike me again.
On one hand, I wanted more than anything to chase the fear away and live again, and on the other hand, I reminded myself of it. I was going nuts with these back and forth thoughts.
I learned that if you chase away the thoughts and fear of the panic attacks, that they will go away.
I had trouble with that because I didn't have thoughts of that when it first happened! In fact, I never even HEARD of it before, so how was my fear of them causing them?
Ok, maybe my fear of them "now" causes them, but what about before, when it first happened?
This came out of the blue.

One thing I was always thankful for were the things I did before I became housebound.
I was glad that I did so many of the things I did, and I had those memories to go to and that helped keep me sane.
My memories and my music were all I had. And my Petie.

It seemed that when something was brought up, I could say I had done that a lot of the time.
I could drive a standard, ride a motorcycle, went snowmobiling, hunted, fished, lived in the country, drove a boat, canoed, etc.....I had done most in my young years that some have never done.
I had those memories and experience, so I was thankful that I knew what these things were like.
When something would be brought up, I could go back to my memories and remember what it was like.

If I could give any advice to anyone, I would say "Make memories, for we never know what tomorrow holds".
My memories became very precious to me. I held on to them and relived them so many times in my mind. That is one thing nobody can ever take away from me.
No fear, anxiety, or person can rape me of my memories.

I continued to watch the kids for the neighbors and more and more people would refer me, and I would end up watching their kids too.
I loved doing this and it helped my confidence and gave me purpose.
I loved kids so much, they were all precious gifts from God and without even knowing it, they were helping me. It brought sunshine into my days when they were with me.

I wanted a child of my own so bad. I would dream of what it would be like to be a Mom.
I just knew I would be the best Mom. I could give a child so much love. It was only a dream, but one I would not let go of.

There was a man who worked with my Brother in law who had asked to meet me.
I told them that I would rather not.
I wasn't ready to meet anyone or trust another man.
They said he had been asking for quite some time, but I still refused. I was flattered, but just not interested.

One day he called me out of the blue. We

***talked, laughed a lot; he was a nice guy and had a funny sense of humor.
After many conversations on the phone, we starting spending time together.
He had said he wanted to help me overcome my condition. I was thrilled about this and I learned to trust him and agreed to go in the car with him.
We started out by just driving around the block and looking at Christmas lights. We went about three times a week.
We would laugh and talk and listen to the radio. We made it a lot of fun instead of allowing it to be a tense, fearful time for me.
Also, it can be very boring circling the same block over and over.
We had fun doing it. The more time we spent out there, the more relaxed I would become and we made it a little further each time. Just one house at a time mostly, but it was progress.***

***When I would be in the car, I would try and figure out just what it was I was doing or thinking that was controlling the anxiety and preventing me from going into a full blown anxiety attack.
I tried very hard to analyze this and to this day, I still can't figure out what it was.
All I knew is I was making progress and I was happy.***

I was so grateful to him for taking the time and caring enough to help me. It was making a difference in my life.
I was very tense on the inside and was fighting the anxiety, but still not sure what I was doing in my mind to block the attacks.
It was very exhausting for me in fighting this, but I wanted so much to recover and was so thrilled that I had the help.
It was working!
I would get as far as three blocks from my home and would request that we go back and drive past my house, then back to the last place I made it to.
We back tracked over and over.
He never complained, and it was working!

I think it felt just as rewarding to him in helping me and watching this remarkable progress, as it was for me to be able to go this distance.
It had been 8 long years.

I was seeing different streets, signs, red lights, houses. It was like a whole new world to me.
I was frightened, yet excited.

After working at this for weeks, I found myself near my mother's house which was four miles from my home!

I always had to go after dark, for there was less traffic, and for some reason, I always felt better going at night.
I thought it was a pretty weird thing, but I learned that most agoraphobics are that way and are sensitive to light.
I used to have to wear dark sunglasses, even at night.

I got brave one night, and decided I wanted to go see my mother.
They had moved some years back and bought a new house and I had never seen it.
We went to the door, and when my mother answered the door, she could not believe she saw me standing there.
It all seemed like a dream to me. I couldn't believe, myself, that I was there.

They had been asleep, for it was late at night, but they welcomed us in with tears and hugs.
They were thrilled to see me, showed me around the house, and kept thanking my new friend for bringing me.

When I say they showed me around their house, it was quick and brief. I couldn't stay long, and I practically ran from room to room so I could see it, but had to leave quickly.

I was fighting the panic and still not actually believing where I was.

My youngest sister Ann and her husband lived just two houses away from my mother, so we went to their house too. It was a very exciting experience for all of us. One I am sure we will never forget. That would be the first and the last time I ever saw their houses.

When we were out for our rides, I wanted to try to go in a store. I did go into a convenience store, bought the first thing I saw, and left.
I just had to accomplish that so I could say "I did it!".
In time, I went into a grocery store and bought a bag of potato chips. I was so excited. These things were very hard for me and I was fighting the fear of the anxiety attacks that could strike out of the blue at any time, but I was continuing to make progress.
I went to his house a few times and was able to stay for hours.
We eventually went to the restaurant his family owned, and I went in and saw it and played the jukebox.
We had to go when it was closed, for I wasn't ready to go in when there were

people in there. I didn't do well with a lot of people and crowds.
I was accomplishing so much in such a short time. This was so miraculous to me.
I always prayed for peace from God before I went and while I was out in the car.

I had a terrible fear of getting into a car accident, or the car stalling, getting stuck at a red light, etc... Red lights used to cause me to panic.
I have a real fear of being trapped, stuck, etc.

One evening, we went to the McDonalds drive through.
McDonalds is always a treat to me because when I have a craving for it, it's too bad. It's not like I can just get into the car and go get something.
Well, I was able to go there and order anything I wanted! Wow! Me, at McDonalds!
We ordered from the drive through window and we laughed so hard, we could hardly order. We always had so much fun together.
Even doing the simplest things were fun for us. We made it that way.
I was learning from him that life is all what you make it.
This was helping me tremendously.

I used to tell him what a difference he was making, but I am not so sure he ever knew just how much.

Sadly, our relationship came to an end. I guess I would have to say it was pretty much my doing, but for other reasons, I felt it was best that way.
I lost a good friend, which I truly missed, and my outings were over.

I don't believe in using people, even for the sake of my recovery, so I could not stay in the situation when other things weren't quite right.

I felt that since my family and friends saw that, with help, support, and understanding, I could recover, and that they would pick up where he left off and start helping me in taking me for rides.
I didn't own a car of my own, and even if I did, this was not something I would ever attempt alone.
My stepfather did take me for a few rides and I did really well, but it didn't last long. I guess there was no real reason, and I never asked. Perhaps he was waiting for me to ask again? Not sure, but I was very down on myself all the time and even though I wanted and needed the help, I

always felt I was wasting their time.
I had very low self confidence and self esteem.

I did ask my mother and sisters once in a while to at least take me around the block once for a different scenery. Sometimes, they took me, but not very often.
They got sick of hearing me complain all the time.
I wasn't complaining, I was desperate to recover.
I got further in a car than I did walking.
In a car, I could get home faster if I panicked.

I was still trying to walk to the corner; the one furthest from my house. That's where the corner store was, and no matter how much I needed something, I just couldn't do it.
I tried so hard and would get so mad at myself, but there were times that I went without something I needed because I just couldn't make it there.
I would ask the kids in the neighborhood to go for me when they were available.

The owners of the store even allowed me to open an account with them and pay them at the beginning of every month.

I didn't have much of an income, and I didn't always have money when I needed something.
They were very kind people.

Once in a while my sister, or a friend would drive me to the corner and I tried to go in the store.
In time, I was able to go in, but had to grab what I needed and leave in a hurry.
We had to leave the car running, ready to leave immediately when I came out of the store.
Every time I made a step like that, I was thrilled. I felt like jumping up and down.
I saw a store, and things on the shelves, and I was able to pick out my own groceries!

It wasn't very often that someone would take me, but each time I went, I did better.

I can remember being in the store and someone complimenting me, telling me I was pretty. I cried and told them they just felt sorry for me and I ran out of the store.

It was very hard for me to hold a conversation with people because I thought they were going to notice how ugly I was.

When someone paid me a compliment, I was convinced they were lying out of pity for me because they saw how ugly I was. I was very shy and very timid as well.

Being taught how ugly I was, and how stupid I was for so long, had an impact on me.
I was pretty much brainwashed.
I completely believed it.
I was a waste of time as well, and didn't matter.

Even on Holidays when the family would come over, it was always constant digs towards me. I ended up in tears every single Holiday.

I treated everyone with respect, but it seemed I was never shown any respect.
I was told I couldn't do anything right, I was stupid, my nickname was "Asshole".
It didn't feel too good.

No matter what I did, I was always reminded of these things, and constantly yelled at, even in front of my neighbors.
I spent more time crying, asking what I did, and apologizing for things I didn't even do.

I was the whipping post for everyone, and

I allowed it. I didn't know any better.
Then again, I didn't know any different.
It had always been this way.
I was just worthless.

If I ever had so much as a twinge of confidence in anything I did, someone always made sure I was knocked back down.

Chapter 10

I got a call one day asking me to be on the Maury Povich show.
I had went through that program I mentioned earlier, and through them, the producers of the Maury Povich show informed me that I was the worst case in the United States.
There was one other person, and myself, and I was it, out of the millions of people that suffered with this condition.

They wanted me to do the show to help others because I had been suffering so bad and I was making progress and they wanted others to see there was hope.

At first, I said no, but when I thought about the other people out there who were suffering, I agreed.

I was 27 years old.

***It was taped Via Satellite from my home. I was nervous and embarrassed and tried my best to be confident.
It was very hard.***

***After the show, I received phone calls, letters, and cards from people everywhere. Some people thanked me for having the courage to go on the show because it gave them hope, and some wrote to encourage me, letting me know that they completely recovered and they are confident that I will too.
I was also called by an Arizona newsletter for an interview, which I did.
My story aired on the local news and was also found in the National Enquirer. I was shocked to find out it was in that particular magazine.
I have always been a private person, and when my personal life and most private issues and fears went public, it bothered me terribly.
I didn't want people to think I was crazy. Some had never heard of this condition, like I, myself, never had until it happened to me and I learned about it.
I feared people would think I was mentally ill, even though I learned and knew it wasn't a mental illness.***

The scary part of it all was that strange men tried to contact me by driving to my area and trying to look me up. Some called me on the phone posing as Doctors. It was pretty scary.

I had never been one for attention, and like I said, was very private with my life and it was out there for the world to know. All for the sake of giving hope to others.

Time passed, and it had been so long since I had been out for a ride, I guess I could say I slipped backwards.
Soon the thought of even going that far again was pretty much out of the question. But even if I had wanted to, there was nobody to take me.

There were many times family members or friends would offer to take me to a certain place, but never to work with me.
They knew I couldn't just get in a car and go to the mall, for example, but they would offer things like that. Things they knew I was not able to do.
When I would make comments that nobody wants to take the time to help me, they would say how they offer, but I refuse. I wasn't refusing "help", I was

begging for it. I was refusing to do what seemed impossible for me at the time. They knew the difference.
Meanwhile, the years were passing me by.

I learned, and I was told by experts that they have never heard of anyone who ever had to go through this alone.
They said it was very unfortunate for me and that most people who recovered or are recovering have someone who is their support person and who goes with them, holds their hand when needed, etc.
I didn't have that.
I had myself, and my cat Petie.
I spent every second with that cat.
I talked to him constantly.
He was my companion, my best friend, my boy.
I also had my music that I listened to constantly. I didn't watch a whole lot of television, I mostly had the music on.
I had a large collection of various types of music and I enjoyed all of it. My tapes were never retired for any length of time.

I continued to pray that God would bring someone into my life that would help me. Meanwhile, I walked back and forth outside of my house trying to get a step further, eventually a house further.

I never really felt comfortable going outside when the neighbors were out because I knew they were talking about me.
I always got dirty looks from them and they weren't friendly and social to me like they were amongst each other. It used to make me feel really bad and wonder why, or what it was about me that they didn't like.

My friend Dawn, who lived in New York State, decided to move back to my town. I found an apartment across the street from me that was available for rent and she moved in.
I was excited about this. I had the security of knowing she was right there, and I got to spend more time with her.
She eventually got a new job, so between that and her family, our time spent together was less often, but we always made it a point to meet on Sunday nights after her kids were asleep.
We would meet half way across the street even when it was raining or snowing, then we would hang out at my house until the wee hours in the morning.
It gave me something to look forward to each week.

Sunday night was our garbage night on our block and sometimes when we were outside, the truck would go by and we would talk to the workers.
I recognized one of them as someone I went to middle school with.
He remembered me too.
I didn't know much about him or hadn't seen him in many years, but he seemed very nice and he was a pretty good looking guy.
At Christmas time, we left cookies outside for the workers.

One day, the guy I knew from school came to visit me out of the blue.
He would start to visit more often and we got to know each other pretty well.
The visits continued for about a year and we became more involved.
I cared for him very much.
He was supportive to me concerning my problem, but not enough to take the time to help me get out there and recover.
There was a lot of talk about it, but it never really happened.
He had issues he was dealing with too.
Issues that I will not mention in my writings to protect his privacy.
I supported him the best I could with his problems. It wasn't an easy situation for me, but because of how I felt about him,

I hung in there and always hoped for the best.
Every so often he would talk of having a child. My dream of becoming a mother had never left me. Not for a day. But I said nothing to him about this.
I tried for over three years and nothing happened. I was unable to conceive.
This hurt me so badly.
I kept it to myself, but I bought books on infertility and tried to learn and figure out why I was unable to have a child.

The Lord is very important in my life, and I know we are to be married when we have children, but I knew I had so much to offer a child and I did love him, I just wasn't ready to get married.
Not to any one.
That scared me because of my past relationships and some of those I had seen around me.
I didn't want a man to have that type of control over me, if in fact, the relationship would have gone bad.
I just wanted to be a Mom.

I would pray to the Lord to please give me a child.
Still, nothing was happening.

One night, while I was on my knees

praying and crying; pleading with the Lord for a child and asking Him why…..I realized I was being selfish.
I then told God that I was sorry for being selfish and that I would accept whatever is meant to be.
He knew my wishes, but I would leave it up to Him as to what was meant to be in my life.
I would no longer beg and ask why.
I was ready to accept what was meant to be.
After over three years of trying, it was not likely to happen for me, and I vowed to be ok with that.

My anxiety was worse some days, than it was others. I was eating better, but didn't touch any sweets or caffeine.
I learned that eating a lot of sugar and drinking caffeine products was causing my anxiety to escalate.
When I quit consuming them, I noticed a remarkable difference in how I felt.
The sad thing was, I couldn't eat some things I loved the very most, like chocolate.
In the past, I could have lived off of chocolate I loved it so much, but it wasn't worth how it was making me feel if I ate it.

I still had trouble if I would see an ambulance, flashing lights, or hear a siren. I would panic and call my Grandmother and she would help calm me down.

I still watched out the window a lot for the neighbors to come home.
Knowing they were there made me feel more at ease. Knowing I could call them if I had to eased my mind.
If they weren't home, the "what if's" would strike me and I would eventually panic.

Night time was hard for me.
Once it would get really late, like past two A.M. I knew most people were asleep by then, even the night owls, and that would cause me tremendous anxiety.
There were many nights when I would call the guy I was involved with and want him to come right over. He always did, and it helped me to relax and feel better.

He had a wonderful family. I was fortunate enough to get to know them.

He drove a race car and raced on weekends and they always invited me to go along.
I told them of my problem, and they

understood, yet always let me know I was welcome to go with them if I ever felt up to it. I appreciated that very much.

His mother offered to help me get out and take me for rides. She was a wonderful lady, and I felt good about it, so I went.

We started driving around a few blocks. It had been a while since I was out for a ride, so I had to work my way up to where I could go further again.
She was a very understanding and patient woman, and I felt comfortable being with her.

I was still trying to figure out what it was I did in the past to hold back the anxiety attacks.
It was like a battle within myself.
Fighting myself.
Trying to protect myself from what was going on within me.
Very hard to explain, but I had to figure out what it was that would make me get through those moments when I got more than a few blocks away.

We drove around my neighborhood and expanded in distance. She didn't live real far from me and always offered to take me to her home when I was ready.

At first we drove by and she showed me the house. I was not ready to actually pull in the driveway, and she never pressured me to do anything I wasn't ready for.

We went a few times a week, and the day came where I was ready to pull in the driveway of her home.
Eventually, I was able to go in and actually sit down and visit.
I was so happy.
They had a beautiful home and they were a very close, loving family. I would have this warm feeling every time I went over there.

Once I went to the dairy queen with her and her husband, their daughter and son in law. They all went in, but she and I stayed in the car, for I was not ready to go inside of a public place.

Each time we went, I made more and more progress and I was so happy and proud.
I was also very grateful to her for the time she was taking to help me.
She worked full time, had her family and her home to take care of, and she took the time to help me get my freedom back.

One day we stopped at a Burger King and we sat outside on a picnic table and ate. I was so thrilled that day. I was able to sit there and eat. Outside……in public. I will never forget that day.

I was twenty seven years old. August was nearing, and on the 25th of that month, I would turn twenty eight. That really bothered me. I still wasn't living a life of freedom, still battling anxiety attacks, and the years were rolling by.

On August 25th, I took an over the counter pregnancy test that had a positive reading. I shook and cried, but did not believe it was really true. Two days later, I had a friend take my urine to be tested at a clinic for an accurate result. When I got the call, it was positive.

It had been less than two weeks since I had gotten on my knees and told the Lord I was going to stop being so selfish and would accept what was meant to be.

I was in total and complete disbelief. It seemed there would be no way that this

could be possible.
It was reality, and I was going to be a Mom!

I was afraid in many ways. I wasn't able to go to a doctor, and I tried to find one who would be willing to come to the house. There was not one doctor who was willing to do this for me, knowing I needed prenatal care.
This scared me even more.

When I was in my third month, there was a doctor who did prescribe prenatal vitamins for me.
That was all he could do for me, but I was very thankful.

I took the vitamins and took care of myself, but had no doctor.
The excitement and fear combined was overwhelming at times, but the main thing was, I was blessed.
Truly blessed.
And there were many times I still had trouble believing that I was actually going to have a child of my own.

I met a woman through a friend who had Agoraphobia and we got to talking on the phone.
She said she could only go places with her husband, but never alone.
Agoraphobics subconsciously choose a safe place, and/or person and only feel safe with the particular person or place they have chosen.
It's strange because it's like we are our worst enemy. The fear lies within us, and only we can control it, but we depend on someone or some place else to feel better. And it really works.
It doesn't make sense, but it's what we tell ourselves. We are usually too unsure of ourselves to depend on ourselves to feel better, so it's easier to pick a place or person and find comfort in that.
We don't mean to.
The answer is to learn to depend on ourselves to feel better and feel good.
Sometimes believing in yourself is one of the hardest things to do.
Even knowing this, it was very hard to learn to depend on me.
This is a very frustrating condition. It's not mental, yet, it has everything to do with your way of thinking.
It can be overcome, and knowing this, brings on so much frustration.
You know better, yet, you just can't do it.

Changing your way of thinking, building self esteem and confidence is the key to recovery, yet not an easy thing to do.

The woman I had been talking to, Joan, had shared her story with me. It was nice to talk to someone who could really relate.

She was on medication to help her cope with her anxiety. I, myself, was deathly afraid of medication. If I even saw a pill, I panicked. The thought of actually taking one was completely out of the question for me.
Joan said she would be able to come over so we could meet in person as long as her husband was with her.
I was very excited to meet her and happy that I had a new friend, especially one who understood exactly what I was going through.

They came over a couple times and I enjoyed our visits.

Her husband Jerry was a very kind and supportive person. She was fortunate to have someone like that who loved her and supported her as he did.

After learning that time doesn't take

the fears away, changing your way of thinking and getting out there and doing it is what gets you to overcome this, we decided to take some steps.
Joan offered to take me for rides in her car along with her husband. I felt pretty much ok with it because I knew she knew how it felt and she stressed how she knows that forcing a person only causes their anxiety to escalate more.
The thought of her ever forcing me didn't cross my mind.
Not her, of all people, for she lived in the same fear as I did.

Until I got to know them better and feel more at ease, they offered to have me do the driving for I knew my limits. So, I drove their car around the block and went as far as I was comfortable with for starters.
It had been a while since I was out in a vehicle, so it was almost like starting over again, trying to work back up to that point where I could go further.

After a couple rides, Joan asked me if I would trust her to drive me in their car. I told her that would be fine with me. Even though I already agreed, she sat there and said everything she could think of to convince me how much she

understood because she lived it too and that she wanted me to know she would never ever go any further than I wanted her to and that she would turn right around at any time that I wanted to.

There is something with Agoraphobics that they have to feel they are in control of the situation.
The worst thing to ever do to someone suffering from this condition is try to force them into doing anything against their will, or to cause them to feel trapped. This can chase them back to square one and it makes it harder to trust people again.

I didn't have a problem with Joan because I knew anybody in their right mind, who suffered from this, would never do something like that to another.

Even after reassuring her I was ok with her doing the driving, she continued to try and convince me that she would never do anything to me against my will. She shed tears and even handed me her wedding set to hold. This is how much she wanted me to trust her and she went this far to prove it.
I handed the wedding set back to her and told her I trusted her and knew she would

never try to force me into anything I wasn't ready for.

During our talks and visits, we had discussed our fears and what scared us the most.
I knew that she could not do anything without her husband, so I told her I would help her work on that and asked her if she would trust me.
I said maybe we can back out of my driveway and pull back in while her husband stood outside of the car.
She said there was no way she would even try that without having him in the car.

She expected me to get out there and push myself, yet she wasn't willing to take those baby steps to get better.
I told her when she felt ready, we would do that. I thought we could help each other.

We eventually got in the car to go for that ride where she would do the driving.
She wanted me to try and go up to the next block from my house, turn around and come back.
I agreed as long as that was all the further we went.
I also shared with her that the next street after that was one that terrified me.

I didn't even want to see that street. It was a very busy street with two lane traffic and I was scared to death of it.

She assured me that we weren't going near it anyways; we were going a half block over on my street, turning around and coming right back to my house.

She drove, her husband was in the back seat, and I was in the front passenger seat. I could not ride in the back seat of a car for it made me feel trapped.
I was just thankful I was able to get into a car again at all.

As we drove, I was feeling ok, talking and smiling.
The next thing I knew, we were going past the point that we were supposed to turn around at.
I kindly reminded her, but she kept driving.
Then I reminded her again how we just sat there for a long time discussing the plan and how she convinced me to trust her.
I kept saying "You promised" as she drove further past that point.
Her husband was in the back asking her what she was doing and reminding her that she promised never to do something

like this. He was telling her to turn around.
I kept saying louder and louder, "You promised! You Promised me! I want to go home".
I begged her to please take me back home. She ignored me and the next thing I knew, I was on that busy street that I feared so bad.
My world was spinning, I was hysterical. I thought I was going to die from the fear and terror I was feeling right then.
I remember looking over at the Plaza and there were payphones. I tried to jump out of the car. I needed to get home and I would have done anything to make that happen.
She ignored my pleads, so I started demanding she take me home, while reminding her of how she lied to me.
I was in a total panic, screaming at the top of my lungs.

Her husband finally convinced her to take me home.

When we got in front of my house, I had trouble calming down, my voice was hoarse from screaming and I feared losing the child I was carrying.
There was no trying to comfort me on Joan's part. Instead she was mad at me

and told me I owed her an apology. I owed her?? She said she didn't want to talk to me again until I apologized to her. That was fine by me because I was afraid to ever see her again!!! I wanted to move, I wanted to hide. This woman was out to get me and it wasn't my own paranoia either! This was a very selfish, manipulating, controlling woman. One I hoped never to see again.

I should have taken more of a notice to all of the red flags that had gone up in my mind since I first met her.

Another lesson learned for me.

This was tough, because I was learning to trust people and try and get back out in the world, but my instinct was telling me to trust no one! I was just thankful to be home and that the baby was all right. Thank God.

Chapter 11

I continued to make calls to try and find a doctor who would be willing to come to the house, with no luck whatsoever. Even though I had taken two tests and they were both positive, I still had a hard time believing that it was true. I was going to be a Mom.

When I was in my 5th month, I talked to a friend who knew someone who had her children at home with midwives. I had heard of home births before, but never knew much about it. She gave me numbers of two midwives who work together. They were wonderful ladies. They came to meet me and decided to be my midwives.

Going through my pregnancy alone wasn't really so bad. I was used to being alone in the first place, and I had my cat Petie to keep me company.
The only thing that bothered me is when the baby would kick and I wanted someone to feel my belly and share that with me, but Petie did that often too, for he laid on my belly a lot and when the baby moved around a lot, he would move up and down too. It was really cute.

I assumed the entire pregnancy that I would have a boy because both my sisters had boys.

My Mother and Stepfather bought everything nice for the baby and the baby's room.
They did it all up nice in blue with a bunny theme. Everything was new, carpet and all. I was all set.

I had decided on the name Matthew Thomas. Matthew is a favorite name of mine, it's also my favorite book of the Bible.
If I were to have a girl, which I really didn't think I would, I was going to name her Emily.
Mom had wanted me to name her Tiffany Rose if it was a girl, so towards the end, I

said I would, but I knew it was going to be a boy.
I felt like a million bucks all through my pregnancy.
It was a wonderful feeling, but I feared having a very small baby, for I wasn't very big.

In my sixth month, I was showing some, but very little.

I remember when Christmas came, my family decided not to come over.
They always came on the Holidays since I wasn't able to go to their house's anymore for the Holiday dinner.
I was very hurt, but didn't show it.
I guess I almost felt sorry for myself.

When my landlords heard about this, they invited me to spend the Holiday with them and their family.
Seeing that they lived downstairs from me, I was able to go. I felt like a charity case.
I was embarrassed, but they made me feel very welcome and I appreciated that. They bought me a nice new toaster.

Towards the end of my pregnancy, I cried sometimes because I wanted to keep my

child close to me always and I knew once he was born he wouldn't be safe within me anymore. I loved him so much already and I hadn't even met him yet.

I was two weeks past my due date and I was having some pains.
I had labor pains for 5 days. Something that's unheard of.
My midwives and my mother stayed with me for 3 days waiting.
I remember getting up during the night and going into the kitchen so nobody would hear me because the pain was so bad.
I didn't want to disturb anyones sleep. They said that's what they were there for, but I was always that type; putting others before myself.

All I kept saying through my entire pregnancy and labor was that I refused to go to the hospital, no matter what.

I won't get into every detail, but the pain got so bad and I was scared, so I made the decision to go.

I had a beautiful baby girl who weighed 8lbs. 3 ounces and was 21 ½ inches long.

We came home the same day.

It was rough being in the hospital. I had to fight the anxiety, especially when I first got there.
The elevator was the hardest part, I think.

They did give me shots that kept me calm and sleeping for the most part, so that really helped.

I kept my promise to Mom and named her Tiffany.

While still in the hospital, I was screamed at, called names and treated very poorly by family members…….because I asked to change my baby's first diaper.

I spent the entire pregnancy alone, was told I was not going to push the baby onto them, which I would have never done such a thing, and now that I gave birth, they were trying to make me feel I had no rights to my own child.

My Mother and sister took the baby home from the hospital and I called my landlady to pick me up.

*After the baby was born, I didn't feel important anymore.
I lied there in great pain and didn't get to see or hold the baby much.
Sometimes when I asked for her, I didn't get the nicest response.
I felt so lost and empty.*

*She was with me all those months and now I was lying there alone.
I wanted to bond with my baby, hold her, feed her, bathe her, get my picture taken with her.*

*I was pretty sore and it was very hard for me to get up and around. I couldn't even shower myself, I needed help.
Nobody was paying any mind to me at all.
I was spoken to with disrespect and my Aunt would come over to help me shower.
Otherwise, I just lied there, other than the visiting nurse that came to check on me.*

*Sometimes I would try to get up and make my way to the dining room where they had the baby; as soon as I made it there, they would take the baby in the other room.
They were purposely keeping her from me, and if I would dare ask to see her for a minute, I was yelled at and treated badly. I bit my tongue.
My older sister stayed over a few nights*

and kept the baby with her on the couch. Oh how I wanted to bond with my precious child.

It was bad enough that my older sister asked me to "give" her my baby when I was in my 8th month of pregnancy.
I thought it was some kind of joke.
She wanted me to give the baby to her and her boyfriend, and told me I could always have more kids. This sickened me.
Of course, I said "no way".
I was still pretty weak, but that was one area where I would not be controlled or manipulated.

The day came when I was able to get up and around pretty good and was able to care for the baby myself and we didn't need anybody staying with us anymore.
I treasured every moment with her.
I still do.
I had the most beautiful baby girl!

My anxiety had gotten so much better. I was eating good and not panicking all the time.
I treasured every moment with my daughter. I had her to focus on and she

grew to love music just as much as I did!
It was her and Petie and I.
We were a family.

I couldn't understand why these people were always trying to hurt me, control me, and manipulate me.
I felt just like a puppet, and had a real problem speaking up for myself.

It was a long time before I had the opportunity to get out for a ride again.
There were a couple people that were willing, but when I didn't get real far after a few rides, they gave up on me.
I guess it was hard for people to understand that I had to take "baby steps".

I continued to pray for someone to come along who had the time, patience, and understanding to help me.

When the baby was six months old, we moved to a new home.
Just like the other times I moved, I was not able to go see the place first, so they videotaped it for me; the drive to the new

house, and the outside of the house. It was a beautiful home and I was excited to get there, yet scared to death. I spent a couple weeks biting my fingernails; something I never do.

When moving day came, they put all of my belongings in the new house and took me last. On the way there, I was feeling very nervous. This house was a lot further away than I had been imagining and my anxiety was getting the best of me. Less than half way there, I started to cry and felt I was going to panic. I asked my sister to pull over for a minute and I remember looking back at the road towards my old apartment, my safe place, and remembering that my stuff was gone, and I can't go back there now. Then I looked ahead, knowing that the new place was still a ways away, and my belongings were there, but I didn't know if I could make it. All I knew is I had to get somewhere fast, for I felt a full blown panic attack coming on. I was so confused at that moment. I felt trapped, unprotected, and very afraid.

My sister asked me if I was ready to

continue our journey to the new home and I just couldn't bring myself to give the final "go ahead". I just sobbed.
Finally she continued to move forward, and I don't even remember the rest of the ride there, but I did get there ok, and when we went in, I tried to focus on looking around and admiring this nice home that we would now live in, still, every second, battling the anxiety.
It did help to see my things there when I went in. I had to keep trying to convince myself that I was home now.

My anxiety never did ease up.
I fought it every second of every day.
It came down to me having to have someone stay with me all the time.
I could not be alone there.

I would get so mad at myself.

I loved the house, the surroundings, and the view outside, but I could not be calm there.
It was too far from the area I was used to being in for so long. After all, I lived at the old place for eight years.

I was very afraid of change. I was learning how change is good, it can be healthy, and I was trying that, but it only made me worse.

I had a male friend who had helped me out a lot in the past with groceries and things, and he told me his new girlfriend was willing to come and sit with me sometimes. They didn't have a car at the time, so he brought her all the way out in a Taxi cab.

I was so grateful for him to ask her this and for the fact that she was willing without ever having met me before.

She was pregnant with her first child, and we talked and got to know each other.

I was embarrassed that I had to have someone stay with me, all the while feeling guilty for wasting their time, for I always thought I was a waste of time, but I was so desperate to not be left alone.

In time, it became harder for me to find someone to stay with me, and we ended up putting an ad in the paper.

I got many calls.
I interviewed people and chose a young woman who was very nice and down to earth.
She started staying with me during the day. I wanted so bad to be able to stay alone and live a normal life and enjoy this beautiful home I was living in, but I couldn't.
If someone was there, I could function normally.

I decorated the house real nice, cleaned, cooked, and spent my time with my daughter, I was so thankful for her. She was the greatest gift. I treasured every second I spent with her. I took many pictures of her and rented video camera's quite often and video taped her.
She was my whole world.
After having her, I couldn't imagine life without her.

I was hoping, in time, I would get used to the new house and learn to become comfortable there, but it wasn't happening. I even phoned my old landlords and asked to come back.
I was desperate.
Unfortunately, they already had a new renter and I couldn't go back.

Every day was filled with anxiety for me and it was a real struggle to get through each day.
I looked in the newspaper for places for rent that were close to the area that I had just moved from.
I found a house for rent, and was able to get it. I was happy, yet scared.
Here we go again, another move.
But, it would be a move closer to my old surroundings.

Again, I didn't get to see the new place until all my things were there and they took me last.
To be totally honest, I can't remember the move. I don't remember the ride there, or when I first arrived at the new place.

The house wasn't as nice as the one I just moved from, but I had some relief because I was closer to the area where I used to live.
I do recall drinking a lot of water when I got there because the house that I had just moved from had well water and it made me gag to drink it, so I had no water for a long time.
I guzzled down glass after glass of that cold city water. I never appreciated water more than I did then.

I got myself settled in and kept busy. I was alone sometimes, and got through it, but I didn't like it.
I would always pray that someone would show up to visit me, so I could relax even for just a short time.

It did get better, but I never had total comfort.

I did get to know the neighbors and it helped me to know when they were home. I knew they were there and could call them if I had a real "problem" with my anxiety. I knew they would help me.

Help me? What could they do for me? I didn't really know; all I knew is if someone was there for me, the anxiety subsided.

Agoraphobics tend to choose a safe place and/or safe person and that particular place or person really does make you feel better.
We make this choice subconsciously, and when we are near this person or place, it works! We do feel better. The mind is a very powerful thing.

As much as I thought I was alone in this, I was finding out more and more that there were millions of people just like me. They felt the same way, and went through a lot of the same things that I was going through.
Some still suffered, and some were completely cured! That was the best part of all I was learning about; this can be overcome!
I was never going to give up.
I wanted my life back.
My freedom.

I had trouble going to the end of the back yard.
I was responsible for the yard work and the mowing and I always loved doing yard work.
My Mother and step father gave me a real nice lawn mower, but I made up excuses all the time of why I didn't mow the lawn.
I was getting nervous.
Going too far into the back yard from the house made me nervous, the heat from the sunshine made me nervous, I was a mess.

Why couldn't I just do the things I love to do?
I asked myself this question a lot.

It was very frustrating, and at the same time, embarrassing.

I wanted to love life, be a confident person, and enjoy the things I used to be able to do once again. I couldn't understand, if I wanted it that bad, why I couldn't do it.

The nights became harder for me to be alone and the couple next door to me offered for us to stay at their house to sleep. I felt so funny, but I was desperate and I graciously accepted.
All I had to do was call on a "bad" night and we could go sleep on their couch.
We stayed there many nights.
I wanted to be home in my own bed, but I was afraid to. It made no sense, but the fear was very real.

Our neighbors had a disabled daughter that we became very close to. She was in a wheel chair and had to be fed and cared for by her parents.
In time, I started caring for her when they went places.
I enjoyed it and it helped them out.

I was a good care taker and very responsible, so why was I such a helpless baby other times?
I knew I wasn't crazy, although I felt I was a lot of the time.
The more I read on this condition, I learned for a fact that I wasn't, and I wasn't alone in this, and the fact that it could be overcome made me never lose hope.

One day some people knocked at my door from a church; they asked if there was anything they could do for me.
I guess they had been going to all the doors in the neighborhood, but it was a Godsend for me.

I shared my situation with them and their Pastor called me.
He was such a kind person.

He talked with me and I shared with him how I was staying close to the Lord, yet struggled with my faith.
That true faith, where you completely depend on God to get you through anything.
I would go so far, and that fear would take over and I would pull back.

He assured me that everyone struggles with faith sometimes and we have to keep practicing it and we will grow.
I wanted that faith, not just at moments, but all the time.
If you have faith the size of a mustard seed...........I wanted that and to keep it.

The Pastor told me that he announced to his congregation that I needed someone to take the time to help me on getting out.
He told them all I needed was someone I could learn to get to know and trust and to take me for rides in the car.
He told me he announced it a few different weeks and was saddened to tell me that there was not one volunteer in the whole church.
I was not surprised.

One day he called me and told me there was a woman who came to him and wanted to help me.
I was so grateful.

I got to know her and she did take me for rides.
I made some improvements over the time we did spend going, but nothing real major.

We became good friends, and I am thankful to her for the time she took to this day.
I don't see her as often now, for she got married and life became busier, but she will always be my friend.

One of my relations told me that their Pastor heard about my situation and felt he could help me.
I was very excited about this.

I met him and shared my situation with him and trusted him because they thought so highly of him.

He told me that he wanted to meet with my father and I because he felt my father should be more involved in my life and do more to help me recover.

After I got my condition, my father wasn't around much. We used to be so close, and since I got the condition, it seemed I rarely ever heard from him or saw him.
That was very hurtful.
Yes, I was less than perfect, but what if everyone had abandoned me?
I felt alone enough as it was, but at least

my Mother was always there for me.
I got yelled at a lot and put down, but didn't have to go without, and they did visit me.
I had nobody else.

The Pastor told me that he had tried to contact my father several times, but never got a response.
He also told me that he would ride by my father's house and saw that he was home, but just not returning the phone calls.
He said my Father and his wife were liars.

I felt pretty bad that Dad would do this and I was confused, but I believed everything the Pastor told me.

Meanwhile, he introduced me to a woman from the church and suggested that we do Bible Study together once a week at my house. We were both thrilled about it and couldn't wait to get started.

The three of us were going to go for a ride together with the Pastor driving.
When we went, he wasn't as understanding as he had pretended to be and he forced me to go further than what I wanted.

After the ride, he apologized and said he

was wrong.
The woman who went with us told him if he had treated her the way he treated me in the car, she would have slapped his face.

I was so timid and thankful to have the help, that I let it go.
She was starting to see something that I was not yet seeing, and the Pastor told us we were forbidden to do the Bible Study and we were to never speak again.
I refused to obey him on that and she didn't know what to do.
I felt he had no right to tell us that.

She became physically ill over the stress that he was causing her when she would see him in church over this.

He took me for a few rides with just my daughter and myself and would talk about how he used to sneak things from his wife, like smoking, and how he was going to give the car we were in to his daughter and get himself a new one. He said why should he care, for the church pays for it anyways.
I did not like that remark.
I felt creepy every time he was around, but I wanted to get better so bad, I kept brushing it all off and thinking maybe I

was making more of it than what it really was.

***He finally set up a date for my father to meet with us.
He told me that the only way I would get better is if I said everything to my father, word for word, that he told me to say, and if I didn't, I would never recover and he would refuse to help me any longer.***

***He told me when my father came, that I was to stand up, and walk over to my father and point in his face and repeat the words that he told me to repeat to him.
I was to tell him how he is never there for me, etc…
I cried and told him I could not do that.
I didn't want to say hurtful things to my father for one, and besides that, I was afraid of my father and had never talked disrespectful to him, and I felt by my saying those things to him, that I would be being disrespectful.***

***Well, the day came and my father was sitting before me and the Pastor kept pushing it and telling me to do what he told me to do.
I was crying and shaking and walked over to my father and started to speak…………
just then, the Pastor interrupted and said***

"Listen to her ……….woe is me, woe is me." And he chuckled as if he was making fun of me!

I said "But you…" and he interrupted again, cutting me off and making fun of me.
I kept trying to tell him how he told me I had to do this, but he would not let me get a word in edgewise!
Finally, my father told me he doesn't have time for me and got up and walked out!
I was shocked and hurt.
The Pastor lied to the both of us.

I started wondering if he had told my father to say that to me and walk out.
Was he playing us against each other?

He introduced me to a lady that was a recovered agoraphobic and told me she was going to take me for rides.
I thought that was my ticket, because she had been through it and would never do anything to hurt me or try to force me into anything.
If you've suffered it, you wouldn't wish it on anyone, or cause distrust.

We went for a couple rides and I felt real

good about it. She was a very sweet person and I really trusted her.
I looked forward to our next ride.

Meanwhile, one evening, 22 people from that church came to my house to pray for me.
They said they were there to pray the fear away.
I certainly believe in the power of prayer and was touched that they all took the time to come to my house and pray with me and for me.
The next thing I knew, one of them took my daughter into the bedroom, and the Pastor seated me in the middle of the living room floor and all the people were seated around me.
He was looking at me and talking to Satan!
I was very confused at this point.

I figured out that he was trying to perform an exorcism on me! He just kept looking into my eyes and talking to Satan. I was scared to death! Then he told me my eyes were glowing red.
When he was leaving, I followed him to the door asking him "why" he would say my eyes were glowing red. He ignored me and kept walking out the door.

I knew I was not of the Devil just because I had fears, and this man was trying to make me believe that I was.
I followed him to the porch and demanded that he tell me why he would say such a thing to me.
He finally responded and told me my eyes were red from crying.
Yeah, that was more like it.

I just couldn't believe he would try to make someone believe such a thing, so I wasn't about to let it go until he admitted the truth to me.

I went for another car ride with the lady that had been taking me. The recovered agoraphobic.
After I reached the point where I felt I needed to turn around and head back, for I had pushed myself far enough, she kept going!
She had promised me and so had the Pastor that something like that would never happen!
I was in disbelief.
I kindly reminded her, and she still kept driving.
By then, I was panicking and begging her to take me home.

She finally pulled over, but did not turn around to take me home. She sat there while I cried and begged, panicking, hitting my head against the window, thinking I was going to die.

Eventually, she took me home, and when I reminded her of how she had promised me and asked her why she would betray me like that, she told me the Pastor told her she had to do that.

Some people look at Pastor's like they are God themselves and this lady was one of them, and she said she had to do what he told her to.

I called the Pastor crying and still shook up and told him what had happened. He laughed at me and admitted that he told her to do that to me. I was in disbelief.

From then on, that Pastor would call me every so often from the church phone and ask me if I was miserable, and when I said "no", he said "Oh, that's too bad, I was hoping you were miserable".

I asked him to stop many times, but he kept calling and harassing me, usually right before he went to the Pulpit to preach.

I talked to a couple people about all that had happened, then he called me and told me to stop telling people for he could lose his place in the church.
I told him to "stop" doing it then!

I finally told my family member of what was going on and all he had said and done and they didn't believe me. I got yelled at for saying such things about their Pastor.

I prayed for the next ten years that they would see the truth and get away from that Pastor. I hated knowing they would sit and listen to him preach on Sunday knowing he was evil.
Well, ten years later, they saw it for themselves and got away from him and fast.
I was thankful to God that they did. I will never forget that.

Chapter 12

I started having chest pains and it was scaring me. I knew I was young, but I also learned that stress can kill you.
In fact, at the time, I learned it was the number one killer in America. Pretty amazing.

I learned that when you have an anxiety disorder, such as myself, even though at times you feel you may be dying, when an anxiety attack strikes, you won't die, it eventually has to stop.
But, if you have this, and you don't overcome it, and it goes on and on over time, it can kill you.
Worry and anxiety can cause cancer, allergies, and death, so when I was getting the chest pains, I became very worried about it.

I knew I couldn't handle going to a doctor, and I already knew from when I was pregnant that there was not a doctor who would make house calls.
If they wouldn't come for the sake of an unborn child, they weren't going to come for any other reason either.
This was very scary for me.

Frank and I still talked and he came around sometimes.
Things were better now between us.
We were more on a friendship basis and were starting to realize that we could never be any more than that.
I loved him, and knew I always would, but I also came to the realization that we could never be a couple again.
In time, I learned to forgive him for all the hurt he put me through. It was bad, but I knew he was sincerely sorry and that it would never happen again.
I truly knew in my heart.
We became closer than we had ever been.
It was wonderful being his friend, and we are still very close today.

When he heard about my chest pains, he became very concerned and called his

doctor on my behalf and requested that the doctor come to my house and check me out.
I couldn't believe it when I found out the doctor said he would come!

When he came, I had someone with me, for I was petrified of doctors and also afraid to find out if something was in fact wrong.
He checked my heart and told me it was anxiety and that I was too young to have a heart attack.
I know you are really never too young, but seeing that I did have this anxiety disorder, it made sense to me that it was anxiety. Not that that's a good thing.
He also informed me that I had better take the measures to do my best to overcome it.
I assured him of how hard I try and how far I have come already.
I was no longer sleeping in the closet, and was able to be alone sometimes and I was eating so much better.
I worked hard to get that far.

He said if it prolonged, it would eventually kill me.

Having an anxiety attack won't kill you, but to have that stress and worry consuming you, for so many years, it does take a toll on the body and can eventually kill you.

I lived in that house for a year when I got a letter stating that the owner had passed away and I had an option to either buy the house or move.
I had no money to purchase a home, although that had been the Impossible Dream for me, so I would have to move.
I had thirty days.

Naturally, I panicked and cried.
"Here we go again".
How was I going to handle another move, and what if there wasn't a decent place available in the area?
This was not good.

My daughter was a year old and we were about to uproot again. Move to a place that I won't even see prior to the move AGAIN. This was so scary.

I searched the newspaper ads for apartments that were affordable with my low income, yet decent and in a good neighborhood.
I found a place that fit all that and my family went and looked at it.

They said it was a nice place, and I was able to rent it.
I didn't have very far to move this time. Maybe four blocks, yet, this was still trying for me.

It really was a nice place, the cleanest place I had ever rented.

We got settled in, but I still had a problem being alone.
I got to know the neighbors and felt better when they were home, just knowing they were there.

I met a girl who lived across the street that was also an agoraphobic.
I couldn't believe how much we had in common.
She was nice and fun to be around.
She could go more places than I could, but she had a lot of fears.
It was amazing that I had never heard of this condition before, but once I got it, I learned of and met more and more people who either suffer from it, or were recovered.

The landlord's brother lived in an efficiency apartment behind me. He had

access to my apartment across the hall
from his, in the hallway.
Sometimes, he walked right into my
house.

I was finding our belongings coming up
missing, and I told the landlord about it
several times.
I was not comfortable with this going on.

Then we found that the furnace was a
danger, and the gas company said it had
to be fixed within ten days.
The landlord didn't comply.
I had to make the decision to move out.

I did not want to, but it would be for
our own good. I was only there for eight
months.

I did find an apartment fairly quickly.
It would be seven blocks away.
Once again, I didn't see the apartment
until all of my belongings were there and
they took my daughter and I last.

When I got there, I was overwhelmed.
They had thrown our belongings in the
house very carelessly, and there was
barely a path to walk through the place.

Then they told me they would never help me again.

I was afraid, and nobody wanted to stay with me until I got used to it, so I asked a guy I had known through my old landlords if he would please stay there for the night. He did and I was very grateful to him.

My daughter was two years old at this time and I was spending as much time with her as I could, and trying to put the place together and make the new apartment a home for us.

It didn't have much of a yard.
Well, it was a large yard, but no grass.
It hadn't been kept up in years, it seemed.
Very un level, and all dirt, along with broken glass, half buried clothing.....it was a mess.
My stepfather came over and we rotatilled the whole area, planted grass seed, added fertilizer and made a very nice yard.

He did a lot for us. Once I moved out of the house, things got better between us. He even admitted once how much he despised me when I was younger, but he was so proud of who I had become as a person.

I only wished he had seen me for who I was back then, but at least now it was better.

He and my mother bought everything for my daughter, and so much for me. We never went without, and then some.
I was always grateful for that.

My Mother took my daughter to all of her appointments and to visit relatives, to the zoo, beach, etc.
I was glad she got to go and do those things, but I had a problem every time she left.
When she would go, I was happy that she was going and could have fun, but I felt lost without her.
I panicked and felt worthless.
She became my purpose here on earth.
I was her Mom, and without her, I had no purpose.

I had to find someone to stay with me every time she went somewhere. I had a panic attack every time she left, and I would either pace or just sit there feeling worthless until she came home.
I wanted to be ok, but I wasn't.

It was hard finding someone to come over and sit with me.

Sometimes, I practically begged for somebody to come.

I prayed a lot.
I wanted to feel normal again and get my freedom back.
I would sit and daydream, picturing my daughter and I going somewhere and enjoying life.
It was all just that, daydreams.

I even cried the first time she went to the zoo; I was happy she went, but I wanted to be there the first time she saw a monkey, an elephant, etc. I wanted to experience everything with her.
I loved her so much.
She had become my entire world from the moment I found out she was going to be in my life.

I continued to read self-help books, books on Agoraphobia, read my Bible a lot, and prayed.
I knew only the Lord could get me through this, and I was leaning on Him the best I knew how. But, I also knew, on the inside, I was struggling with the faith

I needed to see me through.
I can't say I ever doubted the Lord, I was just so consumed with fear, that I was afraid to give it all to Him.
I held on to the what-if's all the time.
What if I panic? What if, what if, what if……… I just couldn't quit.
I was an obsessive worrier.

A neighbor of mine was seeing a therapist for personal problems she was having, and one day she called me and told me her therapist was very familiar with agoraphobia and he was willing to help me.

I was a bit hesitant, wondering what he could possibly do for me that I hadn't already tried.
How was talking about it going to help me?

Plus, there had been doctors in the past who have told me if I didn't take the medication, they refused to help me.
Besides my fear of pills and other medications, I knew this particular drug was highly addictive and that scared me even more.
If you talk to ten doctors, five may highly

recommend it and the others will say not to take it for you could end up with more problems than what you have now, like ending up in rehab.
Also, I had heard horror stories about it causing hallucinations and other traumatizing things.
Taking it was just not an option for me.

Despite my apprehensive thoughts, I decided to give the therapist a call.

He told me he was willing to help me and would call me to talk and sometimes come to the house when he was able.
It amazed me that someone would volunteer their time for me like that.
He also said he would do it for free because he knew I had very little income.
I was grateful for his offer and accepted.

We talked on the phone weekly and he did come to my house when he could.
I opened up to him and shared thoughts, feelings, and things that had happened to me in the past.
Things that I had never told another person.
When I saw the sadness and disbelief in his face, I tried to assure him that it was ok, because it was only me.

I never mattered.
I was convinced that I didn't matter, and I tried to convince him.

This man had a way of making me look at things in a whole different way.
He showed me that I did matter.

For the first time in my life, I realized I mattered. I was somebody.

He even went for walks with me to try and help me get further. I was so grateful to him for all he did for me.
He had a way of making me look at things in a whole new way.
He was the best therapist I had ever dealt with.

Sadly, he had a bout of cancer and he needed to take care of himself, so our sessions came to an end.
He did recover, and I was able to call on him in the future when I was in need, and he always took the time out to help the best he could.
I will never forget him or be able to thank him enough.
It was more than just a job for him, he cared about people.
That was apparent.

*From then on, even though it was a daily struggle, I worked on reminding myself every day that I mattered.
His words kept going through my mind.*

*I had to step out of my shoes and pretend it was happening to someone else.
It was so sad.
If I knew those things had happened to another person, it would have been terrible. Well, I was a person too, and it happened to me.*

*He told me I was stronger than I realized and was lucky to be here.
I said "yeah, most people would have had a nervous breakdown or something".
He said "No,……..most people would have been dead".
I will never forget that.*

*I also learned from him something that all of the therapists had told me all along; to break all contact with all of the negative people in my life or I wouldn't stand a chance of ever recovering.
To me, that was out of the question.
These were people I loved.*

They always told me that even though I loved them, they couldn't possibly love me back, for you don't treat people you love

that way.
They explained how I had to make the decision in order to recover.
It was not one I was willing to make.

Since being at this new apartment, I was having trouble adjusting and being alone at night.
The girl, Julie, that would come stay with me at the other place, said she would come and stay with me at nights.
Every night, she took a cab to my house with her daughter, and stayed with me.
I needed her so bad, and was amazed that she took the time to do this for me.

Her boyfriend, who introduced us, got them safely to my house every night so I didn't have to be alone.
They sacrificed a lot for me and I am forever grateful.

I never look back and think how silly I was to be that way, because it was that bad and even if I could do over again, I don't believe it would change.
My problem really was that severe and I needed her.

I couldn't imagine being left alone.
It brought on panic.

I spent every minute of every day just praying she would be able to make it that night.
We developed a very special friendship out of the time we spent together.

I continued to go out for walks, trying to get even a step further.
Every little bit counted.
I could walk to the shortest corner by my house, which was the distance of one house away, and that was an accomplishment.
If someone was with me, I could try a bit further, but alone, that was my limit.

The longest corner, at the other end of the block was out of the question for me.
I could only walk two houses.
And crossing the street was out of the question. I was totally petrified of crossing the street.
There was a park over there, and I wasn't able to go even though I wanted to.
I used to get so angry at myself because I couldn't do the things I truly wanted to do.

When the ice cream truck would come by, all the little kids would run out to the truck to get their ice cream, or their parents would take them over across the

street.
I would grab my daughter and hurry towards the curb and stop dead in my tracks………I couldn't cross the street.
I would stand there holding my daughter, wanting to go over and get her an ice cream so bad, but I was not able, overwhelmed with the fear of crossing that busy street.
I would then ask a child or another parent to go get one for my daughter and I paid them to do it.
I was so embarrassed, but I was not going to deny my daughter the joy of getting that ice cream from that pink truck that played the music.
She lit up every time she heard it.

I kept walking every day working on my recovery that I was not about to give up on.
Eventually, I made it almost half way up the block.
I was getting to know more of the neighbors and I even asked a very nice lady to please walk with me down her driveway and back so I could accomplish that.
She was very kind about it and walked with me. I made it and was thrilled!

I was not going to give up, no matter what.
It was very embarrassing to have to ask someone to do something so small with me, but I would have done anything just to accomplish that next step. After all, that would be another step towards my recovery, and what was so small and minor to them, was huge to me.
So, even at the risk of embarrassment, I did what I had to do.

Chapter 13

When I turned thirty, it hit me hard.
Every year that passed was another year of freedom lost.
I would never get it back.
This saddened me so much.
All I had were daydreams of what could be.

My friends of the past called me less and less. Everyone was either giving up on me, or didn't even make the time to call me anymore.
My family stopped coming on Holidays.

Ann was now married and I rarely saw her or talked to her. I tried to keep our close relationship, but it seemed the more time went on, the less we talked.
Whenever I would call her, I detected

coldness, like I was a bother to them, a nuisance.
This hurt me very deeply.
It became that I would only see her twice a year from then on; my Birthday, and Christmas Eve.

We always get together on Christmas Eve. My Mother, Stepfather, and sisters come over and we have dinner and open gifts. I always look forward to that because I get to see everyone.
I am there all year long, and can't get out to see them, but at least I know on that day, I can see them all.
I only wish they wanted to see me as bad. It's clear they don't, or I would see them a lot more often.

As my daughter was growing, I had thought a lot about what I would do when she reached school age.
I considered home schooling her; something I had been against in the past.

The more I learned about home schooling, the more I knew it was what I wanted for her.

In order to home school, a high school

Diploma is required. I did not have mine.

I made calls to the school district requesting to take the GED test at my house, and was turned down.
I called several different people and explained my situation and was told they were too busy to sit in my house all day while I tested.
I asked them why they would have time to sit in a classroom all day, but not my home.

I knew people in prisons or hospitals had the right to take the test.
Once again, I didn't matter.

Wanting to home school so bad, I was not about to give up trying to get permission to take that test and get my diploma.

I called Civil Rights because I felt I was being discriminated against due to my condition, and treated like I didn't matter because I was not able to walk into a school classroom.
Civil Rights took my case.
It took about three months, and I was granted the right to take the test at my house.

When I spoke to the woman who would

administer the test to me, she informed me that it was very difficult to pass. She stated that it was easier to go through the twelfth grade these days than to pass that test.
I knew people myself that had failed it four times in a row, and that was after attending night school to prepare for it.

The woman strongly recommended I hire a tutor.
I told her I couldn't afford a tutor and I would have to just schedule a day to take the test.
She asked me a few times if I was sure, or if I wanted more time to try and somehow study. I told her I just wanted to schedule it and just do the best I could.

We set two dates, for it would be a two day test, from 8:00 A.M. until 4:00 P.M. both days. She also told me I had to have someone in the room besides her and I for protective purposes on both parts.

That was a problem for me. I didn't know who I would get to sit with me.
There was nobody willing.
My mother was going to take my daughter for the day while I tested, and there wasn't anybody to sit with me.

I called different people, and finally, there was a man I had met who lived in my old neighborhood that I had become friends with, and he was more than happy to come and sit at my house for the purpose of me getting my diploma.
I was very grateful to him for this.

I was told to get at least twelve hours sleep the night before so my mind would be fully rested and clear.
I didn't even get a whole ten minutes sleep that night. My mind was going all night, and I was nervous.

I prayed before I started, and I completed each test before the time was up.
I noticed the lady raise her eyebrows a few times at the surprise of me finishing and being ready to go on to the next test.
I took all the time I needed for each test, I did not rush, but was finishing before the allotted time.

I ended up completing the two day testing on the first day, in less than five hours, and that included my breaks and calling my daughter four times to see how she was doing.

I received my high school diploma and it now hangs on my bedroom wall.
I am very proud of it.

My family had a graduation party for me in my back yard that year.
They even surprised me with a cap and gown.
It was very special.
I couldn't believe they did that for me.
It meant a lot.
My Mother was very proud of me which made me feel really good.
It wasn't often when they would be proud of me for anything. I was thirty three years old.

I had dreamed of becoming a lawyer.
I read a lot on law and watched a lot of law programs.
I felt I would make an excellent lawyer, but not being able to go anywhere made it very difficult to get the proper schooling.

I learned of a program that allowed you to train at home and get the education.
I called them and inquired about it.
They would not allow me to do it unless I had a date that I would be out of the house

and able to go places again.
I could not supply them with a date, so therefore, I was denied.
I didn't think that was fair at all. Just because I couldn't go anywhere yet, shouldn't mean I didn't matter and be denied of the education.
But, in their eyes, it did mean just that.
So, I lived with the dream. That was all it would ever be.
I had wanted to get the education at the time, so when I did get better, I could get into that field, because I knew when I finally did recover, after being in the house so many years, I wouldn't want to spend it in school.
I wanted to enjoy life again, and catch up on all the fun things I had been missing for so long, plus, have a good job to be able to get by.

Here I was in my early thirties, and I still wasn't over my condition yet. Every year that passed was another year of freedom lost.
One that I would never get back.

Not only did I lose years of freedom, but I lived with this fear inside of me constantly.

I did my best to keep a smile on my face and try to appear to be ok, but I wasn't ok inside.
I was tormented constantly.
Watching the clock all day long, dreading the nights.

I will never forget what my friend said the day I was taking my GED test.
I was in the bathroom, but I heard him talking to the Test Administrator. I heard him say, "Even though Kara suffers with this terrible condition, she always keeps a smile on her face, she is such a nice person".
Overhearing that, made my whole day.
It was the truth. Even though I was suffering terribly on the inside, I always tried to appear to be all right and I was always pleasant to others.

I hadn't heard from Matt in quite a while.
He had gotten married, moved to another state, and had two children.
That was the last I knew.
He always called me every 4th of July, no matter what, because that was the day we met.
I had gotten my phone number changed, so he couldn't call me anymore, and I had

no way of knowing how to get a hold of him anymore, although I thought of him a lot and wished him well, and always had the memories which really came to life every year on the 4th of July.

Some of my fondest memories in life revolved around him, for that was the last real fun I had before becoming home bound with my condition.
All the fears in the world could not take those memories away from me.
They were mine to hold on to forever.
My freedom had been taken due to fear, but not my memories. I truly cherished them.
Matt was someone who always made me feel like I mattered, no matter what.
I made the wrong decisions in life, took the wrong paths, and he was always there to offer support, yet never judging me.

I can imagine there were times he must have felt like shaking me and trying to talk some sense into me, but he never did.
He was just always there for me, allowing me to learn and grow on my own, yet being there if the need be.
I always appreciated that in him.
This was the person I experienced love with for the first time.
We learned it, and experienced it

together. Surely he hadn't forgotten me either...........

I missed him.

Someone I knew from school rented the apartment next door to me.
I never knew him well in school; just enough to say hello when we passed in the hall.
We got to talking and he invited my daughter and I over.
He had a roommate and they both had young sons. They said the kids could play together and have fun.
We would go over and it was fun.
We watched movies, listened to music, and the kids played.
It was nice for me to have something fun to do that I was able to do.
Since they lived right next door to us, it wasn't that hard for me to adjust to being there.
I did have a problem with the front door being closed and latched though, due to my fear of being trapped.
They understood and always tried to make me feel comfortable.

During some of our phone conversations, I used to talk about my past relationships and told him I didn't want to get involved with a man again, or at least not for a long time.
It wasn't something I was willing to consider until my daughter was grown.
I didn't want to risk her having upset in her life because of a relationship of mine going bad. Just wasn't something I was wanting to risk.
I remember him telling me that I was being unfair to myself and depriving myself of something good. He said one day my daughter would be grown up and gone and I would be left alone.
I still stuck to my guns.

He made every day fun. Renting movies, having us over for dinner, etc.
Before I knew it, we were spending all our time together.
He had been in a bad relationship himself and had been cheated on. I felt bad for what he went through.

When I realized he was really feeling close to me, I reminded him that I did not want to get involved. I needed to focus on getting better and wasn't willing to risk the stress of a relationship.

He told me he didn't care about my problem, that it had no affect whatsoever on who I was.
That made me feel good.

He was pretty persistent, and before I knew it, we were involved.

He always did the nicest things for me.
He bought me flowers a lot and treated me very well. He was also very good to my daughter.
But I still had a problem. He drank and frequently attended bars.
Sometimes I had to wait until the bars closed to see him.
I explained that I felt I was more important than that and if that was how he chose to live his life, that was fine, but it wasn't the type of person I wanted in my life.
He made the decision to never drink again.

We stayed together, but things were not good all of the time.
How could someone who loved me so much do the things he did?
It was on and off again for many years.

I noticed a lump in my breast and called my medical doctor.
He made an appointment to come to my house and examine me.
He told me it was possible cancer and I would need a biopsy.
I was so afraid.
If something were to happen to me, what would happen to my daughter? I had to take care of myself for her sake.
I was beside myself with worry.
I had a test done and when the lab results came in, they called and told me I had a staph infection.
"A staph infection in my breast?" How could this happen?

The doctor put me on strong antibiotics, something I was scared to death to take.

My boyfriend said he would be there with me for every dose. He was.
I ended up in bed for a month.
He took care of me, my house, and my daughter. He missed so much work, I felt bad, but I needed him.

One day he decided to call my family to ask if someone could stay with me for an hour or two just so he could go do one job and make a little money.
He was turned down.

*Nobody was going to bother with me.
I was thankful to have him.
I was so afraid.*

*Anytime anyone else in the family had something wrong, they called that person daily, went and stayed with them if the need be, took over casseroles, helped with the house, etc..
Not me.
Anytime I had something wrong, I was on my own when it came to the family.
Nobody bothered with me.*

*After a while, the doctor said I was playing with fire and could die, and that I should be admitted into the hospital.
He doubled the dosage of the medicine.*

*The thought of going to the hospital was out of the question for me, but I thought more and more about my daughter and how I wanted and needed to be there for her always. She was the most important thing in my life.
I made the decision to go to the hospital.*

*Thinking back, it all seemed like a dream.
I was so afraid.
My boyfriend promised he would stay with me the entire time and never leave my*

side.
He kept that promise.
I was there for three days.
They pumped me with powerful antibiotics intravenously for those three days.
Nobody came to see me except my boyfriend's parents, my Grandmother, and my sister stopped in because she was there to see a friend and stopped by my room to tell the nurses to give me some mental medication and got me all upset trying to talk me into it.
I was doing fine until she came there and tormented me about that.
The nurses agreed that I didn't need it.
She always tried to convince people that I was crazy, which I am clearly not. I was calm and dealing well for the most part until she came in there trying to push the issue.

I had never been away from my daughter before, and I missed her terribly.
She was staying between my Mother's and my younger sister's houses.
I wanted to see her so bad and they refused to bring her to me.
I was told I was ruining her day by requesting that.
Then I got yelled at over the phone

severely. I got very upset.
They were keeping the only thing I had, what meant the very most to me, my daughter, away from me.

I became hysterical and was going to leave the hospital and go get her myself.
The nurses tried to calm me and told me my daughter could even stay with me the entire time if I wanted her to.
I missed her so much and wanted to see her so bad.
My entire world was spinning.
My boyfriend was even crying at the way I was being treated.
It hurt him to see this.

They finally brought her to see me and she crawled in that hospital bed with me and slept for two hours.
She missed me so much and was so content to be back with me.
We had never been apart before for that long.
She was four years old at the time.

When I needed support the most, and was possibly going to die, they tormented me even more and used what I loved the most to hurt me.
I was in disbelief, to be honest.

When the Specialist came in to examine me, he was very upset.
He asked who diagnosed me.
I answered him, and he told me there was nothing wrong with me!
They pumped me full of those meds for over a month, three days in the hospital, all for nothing!
I was as healthy as could be.

I was so upset, but yet relieved that I wasn't going to die and I could go home.

I never did anything about that, I just wanted to get home with my little girl.

When I called the family to bring my daughter and please give me a ride home and shared the good news, I was told I ruined their day because they could have been doing something fun, but they had to give me a ride home.
I got yelled at, reminded of what a piece of crap I was, and driven home and dropped off in silence.
It seemed the times when I needed the support the most, was when I was treated the worst. But my boyfriend stayed by my side every inch of the way.

I was back home, in good health, and with my baby girl, and that was all that mattered to me right then.

Chapter 14

***I was still trying to work on doing more, but found myself doing even less than what I was able to do before.
His jealousy was taking over and his manipulative ways were setting me back.***

***His family was not helping matters any either.
It seemed I was targeted a lot, tormented, threatened. I was upset all the time.
I kept finding forgiveness, only to set myself up again, each time with the situation getting worse.***

***Living on hope isn't always the healthiest thing, and that's what I was living on.
Each time, hoping it would get better.***

I wanted to get better so bad.

*I even looked into hypnotherapy,
something I never really believed in.
I was willing to try anything.*

*A friend of mine had suggested it, so I called the doctor, and he said he would meet with me to determine if he felt it would work for me. I guess it doesn't work for some.
I was honest with him in telling him I had never really believed in it, but was willing to do this with an open mind, and trust him the best I could.
He said he knew it would work for me and guaranteed my complete recovery.
I was excited.*

*It was very expensive to have these sessions.
My Mother and Stepfather said they would pay for them, and I was very grateful.
There would be no way I could afford it myself.
My boyfriend heard of this and insisted on paying for the rest.*

We were all excited about it, but I was also very afraid.

I was told I had to have someone with

me for the sessions because of the Doctor/ Patient protection, which is understandable.
I called my friend Diana, who was happy to be of support for me.
I didn't see her often, but we always tried to be there for each other.

I was put "under" four times. He said I would remember everything, and I did.
It was really strange.
He took me back to relive parts of my life as far back as five years of age.
He then told me that I had this problem since age five!
I had experienced abuse inflicted upon my mother by my father, and he said it all started then.
Wow.
Since age five.

No wonder so many things throughout life made me extremely nervous.
I guess it was building up all those years, and with the other incidents happening, it just fueled it more, until I became homebound with the extreme fear and anxiety. How sad.

One good thing I learned during my sessions is that my Mother had so much

built up inside of her for all she went through, which had also affected me, that she was letting it all out on me all those years.
I finally understood.
I didn't like it, or agree with it, but I understood.

It actually brought me comfort knowing that.
It wasn't "me" she despised, it was what she herself had gone through.
She was so built up with hurt and anger, and I became the scapegoat.

After one of my sessions, I went to her and told her I understood, and forgave her.
I always forgave her anyways, but I wanted her to know I understood.

No wonder she always apologized afterwards. She never meant to do it.
I guess we are all affected by things differently.
I am not saying it was ok, or not hurtful.
It caused me to have many additional problems and to be hurt and scarred emotionally, but at least now, I understood why.
I asked myself "why" most of my life.

Needless to say, the hypnotherapy did not cure me as promised. I was no better than I was before.
The Doctor even tried to get me to walk outside further and I just couldn't do it.
I cried like a baby.
I could tell he felt bad for me.

He used to call and check in with me between appointments which I appreciated very much.
He was very dedicated to helping me, but I feel he realized in time, it was a tougher case than what he had anticipated.
And it truly was.

I was always grateful for the memories I had in the past. They helped to keep me going.
I could remember back anytime I wanted to and relive them in my mind.
The countryside, the lake, spending time with Matt; talking and sharing our thoughts and dreams for hours….. He was always there for me in the past.
I knew he was happy in his life, and I just wanted to talk with him, hear his voice, tell him I was hurting.
Where was he?
This was someone who I knew always

truly cared.
I wanted to tell him everything I had been through and was still going through.

Every 4th of July, I would think of him more and relive the fond memories we had. My memories were so important to me.

Other people were on with their lives, making new memories. My life consisted of a standstill, only to have the memories of the past to make me smile.

I got out as much as I could and walked.
I finally made it to the long corner of my block.
It took me six years, walking consistently, to make it to that corner.
I was overjoyed when I finally conquered that.

One day I noticed something was wrong with Petie's leg. It seemed a bit stiff, but he appeared to have no pain.
He was purring like usual and eating fine.
Still, I was concerned.

I called my sister and begged her to take him to the vet just to make sure he was ok. She refused to take him for me. I was really crying. My boyfriend and I were in one of our usual arguments and the not speaking mode, so I didn't call on him.

When my Mother got home from work, I told her about Petie, and she came right over and took him to the vet. They told me it was like a stiff muscle, he was in no pain at all, and he would be fine. They gave me pills to give him to relax the muscle and said he would be back to normal very soon.

He was getting weaker, and all I could think of is it must have been the pills doing that to him. He was slowly withering away.

I stopped giving him the pills, but it was too late. My daughter found him in her room on New Years Eve. He had passed away.

I had him for 16 years.

I never really got over his passing away.

Don't expect I ever will.

I had been missing going to church for all those years. I was raised going to church and I hadn't been able to go for many years.
I learned of a church that was on my block, one street down. It sounded like a nice church and I wanted to try to go really bad.
I did ask several people to take me for rides and try and make going to the church a goal.
I got a lot of promises, but it never once happened.

Not having much income, the thought of me ever having a vehicle of my own was out of the question.
It was hard to make the monthly bills as it was.
I always lived on faith. Somehow, the bills always got paid.
I owed that to the Lord.
It just always seemed to work out for me.

Being desperate to recover, and nobody willing to take the time to take me for

rides to work on expanding my fearful boundaries, I did look into getting a car for myself.
I thought about it, prayed about it, and made a call to a small loan company, got pre-approved and started searching for a car.

It finally happened.
I got a car of my own.
I couldn't believe it actually happened.
I was so happy.

In the past, it took a long time before I was even able to sit in a vehicle, let alone go anywhere in one, but I had worked on that and I was able to sit in it comfortably, but I had to have the window rolled down before I even closed the door.
My fear of being trapped was quite strong, but as long as the window was rolled down, I knew I had an escape if something should happen where the car door wouldn't open.

I started venturing out for my rides.
I hated that I had to go alone; I did so much better when someone was with me, but obviously, that was not going to happen.

I drove around my block over and over until I became more comfortable with it. The more I went, the better I felt about it.

My goal was to be able to expand and get further than that block.
I had fears of the car breaking down, getting a flat tire, and especially getting into a car accident.
That was my biggest fear of all.

If I got a flat tire, or the car stalled, I wouldn't be able to get back home quickly. The" what if's" tormented me, but they were things that actually "could" happen, so it was very hard for me to chase them away.

Still, I kept going.
I drove around that same block so many times, that one evening when I got home, the phone rang and it was the Police asking me if I was all right, for they had gotten a call from a concerned person who saw my vehicle circling around the block over and over.
I was embarrassed, but I explained to them how I was trying to recover from my Agoraphobia.
They understood.

In time, I was able to get as far as three

blocks away.
I was very happy about this.
I wanted to do more, but after that limit, it was harder for me, and that was the point where I knew I was going to need someone with me.
I know that nobody could do it for me, I was the one who had to overcome this, but the support is so important, and it makes such a difference to have someone you trust with you.
I asked my boyfriend to go with me on several occasions, but he very seldom went. Only a few times that I can even remember; and when he did go, he complained, and I thought that was odd.

He claimed he wanted me to get better more than anything, but it was starting to seem like he didn't want me to at all.

When I would ask him if that was the case, he denied it, naturally.
But it was becoming more and more obvious.
How could someone claim to love me so much, do everything in the world for me, claim to want me to get better more than anything, yet try everything to prevent me from accomplishing anything?
It didn't make any sense.

He even tried to take my car from me. Said "Hand over the car". It was amazing. That was "my" car!
He also knew if I got too upset, I wasn't able to do well on my outings, so he would always upset me when I was ready to go.
I continued to go every chance I could though. I was not about to give up. I had come too far.

I remember seeing a woman I knew and had talked to in the past who had suffered from Agoraphobia.
A few years back, she had requested a phone call from me through a mutual friend.
I called her and she had described to me how she had been feeling lately and thought she may be agoraphobic.
I felt sorry for her, and was in no position to diagnose, but I felt that she did in fact suffer from the condition.

I referred her to a couple doctors and I lent her some literature that I had.

The more we talked, the worse her condition got.
She finally hit rock bottom, where I once was at my very worst.

I kept trying to assure her that it would get better, but she had trouble believing that, just as I did when I was at the lowest point.
Her family was not being supportive of her either and she felt very alone.

She had three children, and lived with the father of her children. He was not helping her or supporting her. Maybe he just didn't understand, but I knew how important the support was, and I had none either, so I could really relate and sympathize with her.
She was going through hell.

We hadn't talked for some time, and one day while I was sitting on the porch, she stopped by my house. I was both amazed and happy to see her.
She was getting better!

One day I heard she had been in a car accident, and I called the hospital to talk to her. She was badly injured, but was going to be ok.
She told me how well she was doing and that she left her boyfriend of fourteen years, met a wonderful man who was very understanding and supportive of her in dealing with her condition, and she was

doing amazing things again thanks to his support.
She was happy to tell me that she even went to dinner and a movie and stayed the whole time!
I was so proud of her and happy for her, I cried.
She was once at the worst state with anxiety and she had someone who put their heart and time in and she is now living life to the fullest.
She was very fortunate.

Another fact about Agoraphobia is the longer you have it, the harder it is to treat. I am not saying it's impossible, but harder.

I had my condition many, many years longer than she did, and she was very lucky to find someone who was so supportive in helping her.
I am proud of and for her.

I was still going for my rides, and the arguing was getting worse with my boyfriend.
His jealousy was severe, and I was always on the defense.

It would get no better.

I was still waiting for someone to go with me to try and make it to the church.

My daughter was going to attend Bible School there and I wasn't even able to take her.
It was on my block, but her Grandmother, Great Grandmother and Aunt took turns taking her, for I was not able.
I could drive past the church, but to stop the car and get out of the car and go inside the church to sign her in, was impossible for me.
I wanted to so bad, but I couldn't do it.

That Christmas, she was to be in the church Play.
She wanted me there really bad, and I promised her I would do my best to try and come.
I called my friend Julie and asked her to please take me so I could try and go in and see my daughter, for I had promised her I would try.
I just had to try.

Julie came and got me and we went in and

stood in the back, just inside the doors. I saw my daughter up there, but she didn't see me, for her back was turned.
I don't think I lasted more than a minute and I had to leave.
I broke down outside crying, asking God "Why". "Why can't I stay to see my little girl in the play?" I felt I had let her down, plus, I felt I was wasting Julie's time.
I was so full of guilt. It was very hard on me.

My boyfriend started taking my daughter to Sunday School for me. I wanted her to be brought up in the church like I was, and she enjoyed going.
It would be my goal to try and make it there.

One day I got a call, and the Pastor wanted to come and see me.
I was happy that he cared enough to want to come and looked forward to it.
He came accompanied by one of the female Deacons of the church.
We had a nice visit, but I then started to see that he was trying to teach me and lead me towards the Lord. I had to stop him right there and let him know that the Lord was a very big part of my life.

Naturally, he was pleased to hear this.

He wanted to see me come to church almost as bad as I wanted to go.
He told me he didn't care if I came in and swung from the lights, or jumped up and down in the aisle, as long as I came.
He had a cool sense of humor, and he really cared.

The next Christmas, I decided I was going to try to go to the Christmas program again, which my daughter was in.
My whole family was going to be there to see her and I wanted to be there too.

I went with my boyfriend and we stood in the back of the church, just inside the doors.
I was scared to death, but was determined to fight the fear and stay. I was going to make my daughter happy if it was the last thing I did that evening.

I remember my family members looking back and nudging the others at the amazement of seeing me standing back there.
I had to go outside and get air about seven different times, I cried, I choked, the head Usher went and got me a cup of ice

water, some man in the back brought me a chair, which I never sat on, I was just too nervous.
My hands were sweating so badly that if I would have tipped them to the side, the sweat would have dripped to the floor.
But I stayed the whole time!
That was a huge accomplishment for me, and I was so proud, and my daughter was proud to have me there!
I will never forget her face when she looked up and saw me there.
And I was very proud of her for being in the play.

Chapter 15

I didn't see my father very much since I had gotten my phobia. As close as we used to be and as proud as he always was of me, I hardly saw him or talked to him anymore. He would come at Christmas time and that was about it.
At one point, three years had gone by where I didn't see him at all.
I was told he couldn't handle the fact that I had my problem.
That was very hurtful to me.
Was it because I was less than perfect, or was he too hurt by it all?
Surely, he had to have cared.

I struggled with that for years, trying to understand. I would never neglect my child, no matter what.
I had what was considered a disability.

Most people are there for their kids, especially when they have a problem. I just didn't understand. What if my Mother had decided to do that? I would have been without food, or help with my bills, necessities, etc., all those years.

At this point, my boyfriend was doing everything for me. All my shopping, and anything I needed was always gotten for me right away. He truly was a wonderful caretaker. If only he didn't have those other issues, things could have been perfect, but those so called issues were destroying "us", and me. It seemed we weren't on speaking terms more than what we were any more.

I had cut my hand extremely bad and didn't have use of it for about three months. In those three months, the only person that came over was my friend Julie to help me wash my hair. It was very hard for me to do things. I couldn't even open a can of soup for my

daughter.
She tried to help me the best she could, and we would both get frustrated at times and end up in tears.
She had to help me bathe, dress, etc.. It was a lot on her, but she was all I had.

Nobody checked on me or offered any help except my Grandmother. She always offered, but I would never let her do anything. It just wasn't right. I should have been doing for her, if only I could.

Having the condition I did, you would think the family would visit me more, share Holidays with me, call me more, etc.., but it wasn't that way. It hurt real bad.

I had a friend from back in grade school whom I had tried to find over the years with no luck. Every so often I would call information and try to find her.
Well, after all those years, I found her. We talked on the phone and naturally caught up on our lives.
I was very embarrassed to have to tell her about my condition, but before I could, she told me she heard I was on the Maury Povich show.

A mutual friend from school had seen me on it back then and told her about it; so she already knew.
What she told me next about knocked me off of my chair……..she told me that she had gotten Agoraphobia. I was shocked!

At this point, she was much better and was able to travel and go places, but would not drive a car yet and had trouble with other things.
She also told me her neighbor had it and helped her recover.
It was amazing how even more common this was than I thought!
She said when she met her, now husband, that he was very supportive of her and helped her to overcome it as much as she has.
I always thought she had it made in her life. She told me it wasn't always as good as it may have looked.

Then she asked me if my family still treated me bad……..I hesitated and said "You knew?" She said "Kara, it was so obvious." Then she went on to give me examples of memories that she had. She remembered correctly all right.

It seemed that every time I talked to someone who I hadn't seen in years, one

of the first things they would ask me is if I was still mistreated and how it used to break their hearts to see it go on.

I still keep in touch with my friend, and I am sure we always will from here on. We are in different States now, but we have the phone and we share pictures, and she is very supportive to me, even from afar.

I kept on venturing out for my rides, with every intention on overcoming this once and for all.
One Sunday I decided I was going to try to go to church.
I went in, but could not sit in the pew.
I had to stand, pace, and go out for air .
I had to keep the car running out front of the church in the handicapped zone.
I had to know it was there and running incase I needed to make a quick getaway.

It was very difficult for me to go, but I kept going back.

Everyone was very nice and supportive of me there.
I felt welcome.
What a wonderful feeling that gave me!

There were people who cared.

I burned more gas letting that car run week after week, but I didn't care, I was in church!
Standing and shaking, but I was there!

Each time I went back, it got easier for me. It was amazing!
In time, I joined the choir!
I actually went to choir practice on Wednesday nights and sang in the choir on Sunday Mornings!
I had to hold the Pastor's wife's hand while singing in the choir for support, but hey, I was doing it!

I could tell that the more I was doing, my boyfriend was getting bothered by it all. Although he claimed to be happy for me, he felt threatened by it.
I was starting to bloom.
Knowing I needed him by my side to do any of this, he started refusing to stay for certain church functions and would even threaten to leave me there.
That would always get me to leave right away.
As I got stronger, others' would see this and offer to stay with me so I could attend certain things, and I did!
I attended dinners, parties, etc.. It was

wonderful.
It had been so many years.
Nineteen, I believe.
I had done nothing until then.
I didn't even know how to act.
I wasn't completely comfortable, but I was able to attend and stay!

A couple times, he came into the church and told me to go home, that I had been there long enough.
He also hated when I would stand around and socialize with people.
I wish he meant what he said when he claimed he wanted me to get better.
He really didn't. He wanted me to depend on him only, and be right there with him, at home.

Not only was I fighting the disorder, but I was fighting his denied jealousy as well.
That was the last thing I needed, was someone trying to hold me back.

I kept going to church anyways, with or without him.

One day while at church a woman came up to me and introduced herself to me.

She was very nice.
We got to talking, exchanged phone numbers and became close friends.
I was thankful to have met her.
She started being my support person, so to speak. She sat with me, went outside with me when I needed to go out and get air, and befriended me in every way.
The day I decided to be Baptized at the church, she even got into the water with me for support.
It was amazing, and that was an amazing day.
One I won't ever forget.

I was finally able to shut my car off while I was in church, and sit in the pews, but I held on to my car keys every second.
I also could not be behind a closed door.
If we were in Bible Study or if I went into the office to talk to the Pastor, the door had to either be left open, or closed, but not latched.
I was so afraid of being trapped.

The more I went, the more people learned my fears and tried to be as supportive as possible, for example, leaving the door open when I was there.
They were very good to me and it kept me comfortable enough to keep coming back.

I had learned that love and support was so important in recovering, it was the main key.
I was finding that to be true.
The more love and support I was shown, the better I did.

Another 4th of July rolled by, and still no Matt.
I would always think of him, especially on that day, and wonder if he was thinking of me too.
Wondering if he wanted to call, knowing he couldn't because my phone number was different.

One day I was checking my email, as I did daily, and I could not believe what I saw!
There was an email stating that Matt was trying to locate and contact me!
I was thrilled.
I emailed him right away, and he sent me his phone number and I called him.

It was so good to hear his voice again.
He was now single, and had two wonderful children that he was raising.

We got caught up on the time that we hadn't been in contact, and started talking

and emailing regularly.
He was sorry to hear that I was still agoraphobic, and to be totally honest, I was embarrassed to tell him at first.

When we were catching up, he shared what had been going on with him, and it had all been very successful, which I was proud of and for him.
Then I had to tell him I was still suffering with the condition, and of all the bad things that had been going on with me in my life.

I then realized that I never should have felt that embarrassment, for he would never judge me, only feel compassion for the situation and show support, just like he always had.
I was blessed to have him back in my life.

I reminded him, that the last good memories I had in my life before becoming house bound, included him, and that I thought about it all the time.

As we talked more and reminisced, our letters were brought up; the ones we used to write to each other.
We "both" still had all of our letters!
I had all the letters he ever wrote me and he had all the ones I had written him!

We were both amazed.

Gosh, I had missed him.
It was great to have a positive person in my life.
I had no bad memories of him, for he never did anything to mistreat me and never would have.

I shared with him how I believe I could have been completely recovered if only I would have had the support I needed.
In response to that, he said something to me that I will never ever forget.
He said, "If I knew the answer, or what it would take, I would take the time to come up there and do it so you could be better".
That meant so much to me.

He was a very successful businessman and hardly had time for anything, between his business and his family.
I knew he meant what he said.
That's just the way he is; genuine and true.

I continued to go to church and did better all the time.
One day I overheard the Pastor talking about needing someone to do the Church

Bulletin every week.
I stepped up and told him I would be willing to do that for the church if someone would show me what to do.
He immediately said that would be great, and I took it on.
I felt so good having that responsibility, and knowing I was "able", made a difference in my world.
And the fact that they depended on "me" every week to have them all done and on the table.
I finally felt important.
Well, when I was there.

At home, it wasn't so pleasant all the time. I wasn't treated very respectfully by others. I would try to keep the spirit I got in church and hold onto that all week long until I went back and was nourished again.
I talked to the Pastor on the phone regularly and that helped.
I was becoming somebody.

I was always a nobody to so many, and then became that way to myself, but I was starting to learn and feel that I mattered.
All I ever needed was a little kindness.

One day while I was out in the yard cleaning my daughter's pool, the phone rang.
I got a call that made my whole world spin.

Somebody wrote an anonymous letter to the place where I got my income to survive due to my disability, and filled it with lies. Telling them I shouldn't be allowed to have car, that I brag about how much money I have, etc..
I couldn't believe someone could hate me that much to wish me to lose everything and leave my daughter and myself homeless.
I couldn't cope, and thought I had a heart attack.
I had to have an EKG done, and the results showed something wasn't quite right with my heart.
I would have to be hospitalized for further testing to know for sure.

After my last experience in the hospital, there was no way I was going back.

Bragged about my money? I was so poor, I cried a lot wondering how I was going to pay the bills each month.
And shouldn't be allowed to have a car? That meant I would have a slim chance on

*ever getting out.
This all meant to me, that someone saw me making progress, and instead of being happy for me that I was finally recovering, they wanted to destroy it all for me.
To me, that's just sick, but I was still very hurt that someone out there, who knew me, hated me "that" much to want to hurt my daughter and myself.
Shame on them.*

*It all turned out fine though. I was told they wanted me to have a car so I could get better and the rest was all fine.
I had done nothing wrong.*

I just couldn't believe what I had to go through emotionally because somebody wanted to ruin my life.

*That incident made me start looking a little closer at the people around me.
There were many who were cold to me and unfriendly and who gossiped about me.*

*I was even told once by a man that his girlfriend hated me because she thought I was pretty and had a nice shape and he was forbidden to even look at me.
He was apologizing for not being neighborly when I was out.
I told him I never noticed, because I*

didn't! I minded my own business.

Why would she spend her time obsessing about me if she didn't like me?
But to not like me because she found me attractive?
This was becoming the story of my life.

If some of these people paid half attention, and saw how little confidence I had, maybe they would have thought twice.
Then again, maybe not.

I was always told I was attractive, I just never saw it.
But to hate me for it?
I started to wonder just "who" had the problems here.

After the anonymous letter was written, I didn't even want to go out and show my face for the longest time.
I was afraid that if they saw it didn't work, they may plot something worse against me.

I started seeing nails behind the tires of my car, and new scratches on my car.
I had several flat tires.
This all happened right in my driveway.

Somebody was surely out to get me.

Why couldn't people just leave me alone? Smile when they see me progressing, not try to prevent it?
This is something I would never come to understand.

In all these years, all I had were people trying to hold me back, call me names, and abuse me.
I didn't get it.

All I wanted was my freedom back.
I wasn't bothering anybody.
It seemed to me that just showing my face in public caused people to target me.
Why did they have to spend all of their time thinking about me and what I was doing if they didn't even like me?
And plotting ways to be hurtful to me.
This happened a lot.
I was very sensitive and took these things very hard emotionally.
I always wished I was strong enough to not care and just blow it off, but I wasn't.
I was hesitant to even go to church anymore.

I did tell the Pastor and the Deacons of the church what was going on, and they were praying for me and supporting me

the best they could.

My boyfriend and I were apart, but he was also harassing me daily, and it was all getting hard for me to handle.
I was an emotional wreck.
At the time, I saw no light at the end of the tunnel.

I wanted off of that busy street I lived on that I was so afraid to cross, and away from the neighbors who gossiped about me and wished me the worst. I was stuck.

Matt and I talked about him coming to visit us.
We made plans, and he came and stayed for a weekend.
We had a great time. It was wonderful to see him.

His Mom lived with him, along with his twin brother.
His Mom always took care of the kids when he was away, so he was able to break free to come see us.
I was happy that he took the time for us.

He even brought the letters I had written him years ago, and we sat there and read them and reminisced.
We were both pretty choked up when it came to the letters.
We shared a lot of ourselves in those letters.

I continued to share a lot with him.
Whether on the phone or by email, I told him everything.
I shared all my thoughts, feelings, good times, and bad times with him.

One day he told me I should write a book.
I told him that so many people have told me that same thing, and he asked what was stopping me.
I thought about it and realized the only thing stopping me, was me.

Now I am sharing my story with all of you in hopes that if you, too, suffer as myself, please don't ever give up.
Or if you know someone who suffers like me, hold their hand, walk with them, support them.
You can help change a life.

Chapter 16

I am now living in my very own home.
My dream to become a home owner came true in September of 2004, thanks to Matt, who helped make this possible for my daughter and myself.
He said it was the break in life that I always deserved, but never got.
He is an amazing friend.

I am thankful for each step I take in our new home, for I know, if not for him, we would not be here today.

I still have the Agoraphobia.
The only place I go at this point is to church and back, but I am the Youth Group Leader now and I can make a difference in the lives of the children.

How rewarding.
They are our future, and what we do today, affects the rest of their lives, and ours.

My daughter is growing fast. I still continue to home school her.

We have many problems with some of our new neighbors.
We are threatened, harassed, our property gets stolen and vandalized, but we are stronger for it all.

What doesn't kill us, only makes us stronger, right?
And I have found it does.

I am stronger than I ever was.

I am also able to be alone now all the time, and I can honestly say, I can't remember the last time I had a panic attack.

I don't get much company or phone calls.
If I am hurt or sick, I am on my own, nobody really cares, but the Lord always sees me though.

It still amazes me to watch the family run over to each others houses when one is sick or injured, offering their help and support, but not here.

I even fell down the stairs recently and broke my thumb. I set it myself and still deal with the pain.
There was no concern from the family, except my Mother. She always comes when something happens.

Even if a family member has something like a garage sale, they are all over there helping out, bringing food, etc.
I had one every year and not one person ever came to mine, let alone offer a hand.

Right before we moved to our new home, I was cut severely on my foot.
The Paramedics thought I was going to lose my foot.
I refused to go to the hospital because I knew I would be a prisoner once again to the control they had over me when I was weak.
I told the Paramedics I was going to pray and the Lord would heal me.
He did!
Quicker than I had expected.

When I was first laid up, my Mother came over and tried to help with the house and feed the animals, etc. But she was in too much pain because she was having problems, and couldn't do any more.
A couple of my neighbors came over and picked up and did some dishes for me, and my Aunt came over and took my blood pressure.
She and my Uncle were always there to lend a hand when needed, and still are.
Nobody else came or called to check on me.

My ex boyfriend came by and learned I was hurt, and offered to help me out.
I refused at first, but I was so scared and desperate, I accepted the help.
Not sure what I would have done without him at the time.
But wasn't my family the first to criticize my letting him come around?
They sure weren't going to help me.

Shortly after I healed, it was time to move to our new home.
Other than paying my nephew for an hour of his time, and one friend who helped with some of the appliances, I had one person help me.

It took nine days, working nineteen hours a day to get moved into our new home.

Two of the neighbor ladies who I am friends with helped me clean the old apartment and set up the new house, which I was very grateful for.

During the move, there were two of us, and I had no choice but to work like three men. I could not believe nobody would help me. It was very hurtful, but I tried to block it out and focus on our new home, which I could not believe was happening. I was so grateful to Matt for what he had done to make this possible.

There was someone I had been keeping in touch with who kindly offered to help me with the move.
I was grateful for the offer, but felt guilty to accept the help.
As much as I truly needed it, I was embarrassed, I guess, to have him know that nobody cared, and to have him do all that work.

After the long move, I was excited to get the house set up and decorated.

I had planned for so long how I would decorate it.
It was amazing how well I was adjusting.

Anytime I moved in the past, I had needed someone with me for a while.
I needed no one, and that was a good thing in more ways than one, for I had nobody to stay with me even if I needed that.

Hardly anybody came to see our new home.
Some of our family members came to see it, but that was it.
None of my old neighbors, whom I thought were my friends came to see it.

This would be when they mysteriously broke all ties with me, came to hate me, and would never speak to me again.

To this day, I do not know what I did to any of them.
I was always kind to them and never had so much as a disagreement with any of them.
I was saddened and confused, but not surprised.
It had become normal to me for people to turn on me and come to dislike me,

especially when anything good happened for me in my life.
And the horrible rumors that I hear are said about me can be very hurtful.

I continue to keep growing in my Faith in God.
He saw me through so much, and I know He is the reason I am where I am today.

When I look back on everything I went through, I know He carried me through it all.
Faith is a struggle for most every day, and if we try to do it our way, or have doubt, we can fall; but if we do our best to trust and keep our faith strong, we can do anything! I am proof of this.

Always remember to be thankful for what you do have, even in the midst of the hardest, lowest times, and you will be rewarded.
Every time I asked God to get me through something, I always remembered to be thankful for what I did have, for the fact that I could walk, see, etc… He heard me every time.

I know He didn't do this to me, for He

does not give us the spirit of fear, but He does allow the ways of the world, and that is where we are tested in our Faith.
He helps me every single day, and I know that he will see me to the light at the end of this long tunnel I have been crawling through, and the belief in that is all I need to get to the light, so I can be free and fly.

Until then, I will continue to count my blessings and walk with the Lord.

When we were going through extreme hard times after our move, I was crying out for help.
I was stressed out and couldn't believe how much hate surrounded us.
I went to the church for prayer, and went to my family for help.
Nobody knew how they could help us.
We were constantly threatened every time we showed our faces outside.
Our property, and my vehicle were being vandalized constantly, and I didn't know what to do.
We weren't able to enjoy sitting on our porch, going in our yard, I was afraid to let my daughter go out and play, all because of the threats that were made against her.

It was awful.

It finally got so bad that my Aunt thought it was time to call my father.
I agreed.

I was told he didn't want to hear it.
I was so hurt.

I spent four days in bed, crying, unable to cope well thinking of the hatefulness out there and the fact that nobody cared enough to help us.
After the fourth day, my hurt and fears turned into anger.
It hit me that I was our only protector. I had no choice but to be strong.

From then on, every time they threatened my daughter, or stole and vandalized our property, I lashed back.
I went to them, went to the Police, and had no fear from then on.
I had to do what I had to do.
The threats lessened, but I did find a hole in our pool, more dents on my car, a shot windshield, and some days I had to go out and wash the spit off of my car.

I deal with whatever comes now and try

not to let it get the best of me and control me any longer.

I have changed so much lately, some days
I don't even know who I am anymore.
In a positive way.

People are not used to me being aggressive and sticking up for myself, so they tell me I am mean.
Mean?
No way.
I finally know that I am somebody, and I matter.
They can no longer control me, and they don't like it one bit.
They still try to manipulate me, but I will no longer tolerate it.

All those years the therapists told me I had to be that way in order to ever get better, and I didn't know how to even begin to be more assertive or defend myself from the hurtfulness that people brought on to me, especially my loved ones.
I can now say that nobody will ever treat me that way again and get away with it.
I don't need anybody or anything that much where I have to be their puppet, or pay a price with my nerves and emotions.
Never again.

I have but a few positive people in my life, and that's all I need. The Lord will guide me and see me through.

It has been 23 long years now since I have suffered with this condition, but I am finally stronger and more positive than ever before.
I am thankful for what I can do today and hope to reach complete recovery.

It took me many years to learn to believe in me and with that and my Faith, it's all I need.

When I look back on the days where I wasn't even able to look outside, eat, panicked constantly, and was tortured and abused, I am not sure how I survived.
I owe my sanity, the freedom I have now, and my life to the Lord.
It was He who held my hand every step of the way when nobody else would.
I begged and prayed for someone to be by my side and hold my hand through the hardest of times.
I didn't realize it then, but He did answer my prayers, for He was there all the time.

It's still hard being put down a lot, knowing very few care and most of the time feeling like I have nobody, but He is always there.

I am so much stronger now and my Faith is remarkable.
I have pretty much lost all Faith in mankind except for a few, but I walk with the Lord and look forward to the day when I can finally spread my wings and fly.

There are days when I don't know how I will get necessities from the store, etc…
I get embarrassed that I have to feel like I am begging just to get something we need.
It's very hard to find someone to do this for us, but somehow it always works out.

Not sure if people think we survive on air alone, or what.
I feel very neglected at times, but I know the Lord will never leave us or forsake us.

People are just selfish and cruel sometimes, and although I need them, I was finally able to find that medium point where I need them, but I now know I don't deserve to be mistreated in return for what they do for me.
I can stand up for myself, and I do.

I don't think they like that very much.

Every so often they try to brainwash me into thinking I don't look right, should get a breast reduction, cut my hair, etc… just like old times.
I still get screamed at, called names, and told how terrible I am.
I no longer cower to it, or change a thing about myself, or even question it.
Now, I shake my head and LAUGH as I walk away in "my" house, thinking "How do you like me now?"

Final Chapter:

This book was written to share my story with others.
I struggled with emotional and physical abuse, and my Faith.

I couldn't put every detail of what I went through in this book, for it was too hurtful even to write.

But, I want you all to know that if you suffer from this, or any condition or emotional disorder, that you are not alone.
The Lord will always see you through.
I am living proof of this.
He is the answer to all, and the very best medicine.

I may not be doing all I want to in life right now, but I am able to touch God's

nature, feel the sun on my face, the wind in my hair, and I never have to cut my hair again unless "I" choose to!
I will not allow anyone to ever treat me that way again, and believe me, they try every day.
But I am stronger for it all, and I am closer to God than ever before.
People will let us down all the time, but the Lord will never leave you or forsake you.

To My Friends:

This page is dedicated to the people who stood by me and helped me through some of my hardest times.
I will never forget what you did for me.

For all the time you took comforting me, going to the store for me, and supporting me, even when you really couldn't understand, never having been in my shoes.
I thank you for it all, I am very grateful.

And Matt.....what more can I say.......?
I love you.

May God Bless You.

Agoraphobia ***typically results from the fear of having a panic attack in specific situations "from which escape might be difficult (or embarrassing) or in which help may not be available in the event of having an unexpected or situationally predisposed Panic Attack or panic-like symptoms" (DSMV-IV). Literally, "fear of open spaces or of being in crowded, public places like markets" from the ancient Greek agora or market, agoraphobia is generally understood as fear manifested in the avoidance of a cluster of situations such as crowded places, heights, being alone, being in a crowd or standing in a line; being on a bridge; and traveling in a bus, train, or automobile.***

Agoraphobia can lead to extreme anxiety and avoidance, leading some victims to become "housebound," unable to leave a very small "safe zone."

The early treatment of anxiety helps avoid the escalation of symptoms into agoraphobic behavior.

Agoraphobia is responsive to both therapeutic and medical treatment.

About The Author

***The author is a single mother of one daughter, whom she has home schooled Since Kindergarten.
She is also the Youth Group leader at her Baptist church.***

She has appeared on Maury Povich, and has been featured in the Encourage Newsletter, and The National Enquirer.

***She loves the Lord, and some of her favorite things are music, cats, and Caring for and working with children.
She enjoys nature, gardening, bicycling, And playing tennis.***

She has endured a long battle with Agoraphobia, an anxiety disorder shared By millions of people, such as Kim Basinger, Donny Osmond, and the famous Poet Emily Dickenson.

Her favorite quotes:
"Only if you have been in the deepest valley, can you ever know how magnificent it is to be on the highest mountain"

"Be the change you would like to see in the world"

You can email her at: karalynne@usa.com

CPSIA information can be obtained at www.ICGtesting.com
Printed in the USA
LVOW08s0347260816

501917LV00001B/35/P